BEYOND BULK

The Teen's 3 Month Muscle Growth Transformation

MATTHEW RAUDEBAUGH   2024 version

Table of Contents

About the Author

Hello and thank you for choosing to purchase my book! Your support means the world to me, and I'm thrilled that you've decided to join me on this journey. Whether you're here for fitness advice, motivation, or simply to enjoy a good read, I'm grateful for your interest in my work.

If you have any questions, comments, or would like to be notified about my upcoming books, or **CUSTOM** workout plans for a great price, please don't hesitate to reach out. You can contact me at **RaudebaughMatt@Gmail.com** I'm always eager to connect with my readers and share my passion for fitness and well-being.

Matthew Raudebaugh

In addition to writing, I also offer online personal training services. This comprehensive program includes Zoom calls, personalized workout plans, technique videos, and weekly meetings to keep you on track with your fitness goals. I've designed this service to be affordable and accessible, so you can embark on your fitness journey with confidence and support.

Your honest feedback and reviews are invaluable to me. After reading this book, I kindly ask that you leave an honest review on my Amazon page. Your input will help me continue to create quality content in the future and improve as an author and fitness enthusiast.

Thank you once again for your support, and I wish you the best of luck on your fitness journey. Together, we can achieve our goals and lead healthier, happier lives. Stay motivated, stay active, and keep striving for greatness!

Purpose

Truth

Fitness Influencers want you to believe that they hold the secret method. They want you to believe that gaining muscle and achieving your fitness goals is hard. This is a **LIE.** As a personal trainer, my goal was always to equip my clients with the skills they need to be successful and educate them so they can go on their own for **years** to come. **90 days** is enough time to build these principles. Building muscle becomes remarkably simple when you understand the underlying principles. This book is designed as a comprehensive 90-day program, but it's true worth lies in giving you the **tools** necessary to maintain your regimen and stay accountable well beyond on the initial months outlined in this book.

Value

A **month of personal training** can run you well over **$1000**. While you can gain good information its very expensive. I want to give you **a full 90 days knowledge of training in this book.** By the end of this program, you'll possess an understanding of how to continue your fitness journey independently, all for a fraction of the cost of a single personal training session. It's time to empower yourself with the knowledge and confidence to lead a fit and healthy lifestyle for years to come.

Disclaimer

The NUMBER ONE REASON for getting injured in the gym is people lifting far TOO HEAVY. You need to slow down everything that you do and focus on form, or YOU WILL GET HURT. Slowly controlling weights will help you gain so much more muscle vs. cheating your form on swinging weights.

Slow reps keep you safe and maintain tension on your muscles. NEVER swing weights or use momentum, as this indicates the weight is too heavy, and you're not effectively targeting the desired muscle.

Warning

This book contains hard work!

If you think this book will be a **magic method** to easy growth, just like the other outrageous claims on the internet, then **stop reading now.** Seriously!

The 3 Month Muscle Growth Plan is not for those who are looking for a quick fix or a shortcut to a ripped physique. You'll see "influencers" making these claims all over social media. These people are liars. This book is for the dedicated and the disciplined, the ones who are willing to put in the work and commit to a 90-day challenge that will transform their bodies and minds. This is not a book about spoon-feeding you easy solutions, but about equipping you with the knowledge, tools, and motivation you need to achieve your muscle-building goals and push yourself to new limits. If you're ready to take on the challenge and see what you're truly capable of, then keep reading, and let's get started.

Do YOU have what it takes?

Getting Started

Are you ready to embark on a journey that will transform your body and change your life forever? If you're new to the world of muscle building, let me tell you one thing: the gains you'll make at the beginning of your journey are **exponential.** That's right - if you're just starting out, you have the potential to gain an impressive amount of muscle mass with the proper training in just 90 days.

We call this phenomenon **beginner gains,** and it's one of the most exciting aspects of starting a muscle-building journey. But here's the thing: beginner gains don't last forever. Eventually, your body adapts to the stresses of weightlifting, and those initial gains become harder to come by. That's why it's crucial to take advantage of this window of opportunity and make the most of your beginner's gains while you still can.

But here's the catch: the gains won't come with minimal work. You'll need to work hard, push yourself to new limits, and commit to a 3 Month challenge that will test your mental and physical strength. But trust me when I say this: 90 days is enough time to transform your body and your mindset, and set you on a path to success that will last a lifetime, not just 90 days.

In this book, I'll show you how to do just that. I'll provide you with a 13-week-long plan that's specifically designed to help beginners maximize their gains and set a solid foundation for future progress. And to make it even easier for you to track your progress, I've included charts in the back of the book that you can use as your very own workout log. With this plan and these tools at your disposal, you'll be well on your way to achieving the body of your dreams and becoming the best version of yourself.

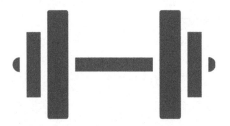

What can I expect from the training plan?

In this plan, I'll give you a workout for each day and week. Each new exercise and workout will come with clear instructions and helpful tips. This will help you not just do the exercises, but actually make progress as you go through your fitness journey. You will graduate this 9 day journey with a new knowledge of how your body works and you will know how to train going forward.

Week 1

- Focus on dynamic warm-up exercises to increase mobility and flexibility
- Introduce basic movement patterns such as squats, rows and chest press, to build overall strength in basic movement patterns.
- Perform high rep sets with light weight to learn form and muscle stability.

Week 2

- Emphasize proper form and technique in all exercises to prevent injury and maximize muscle activation
- Use slightly heavier weights and perform slightly lower (8-12) to focus on perfecting form
- Incorporate core exercises to improve stability and balance during lifts
- Introduce basic compound exercises like bench squat and RDL.

Week 3

- Increase the weight used in compound exercises by 5-10% to challenge the muscles and promote adaptation
- Incorporate drop sets and supersets to increase intensity and promote muscle fatigue
- Perform a few low reps with heavier weights later in the week to stimulate strength gain in addition to our higher rep sets

Week 4

- Begin to incorporate more isolation exercises
- Continue to use moderate weights and perform 3-4 sets of 8-12 reps to promote muscle growth

Week 5

- Perform low-intensity exercises such as yoga, pilates, or light cardio to promote recovery and reduce muscle soreness
- Focus on stretching and foam rolling to improve flexibility and prevent injury
- Drop resistance training to just Two days at a much lighter the load to still get in some form practice

Week 6

- Change the workout plan to 5 days a week after a week of rest
- Continue to gain strength
- Introduce new exercises using various free weights and cables to continue to gain muscle.
- Take a few sets to failure in the end of the week

Week 7

- Increase the number of sets and reps performed in all exercises to increase overall training volume
- Introduce advanced techniques using drop sets on some isolation exercises
- Perform 4-5 sets of 8-10 reps with what used to be to heavy weights but you WILL be stronger by now

Week 8

- Introduce some new isolation exercises to target different muscle groups and prevent plateaus
- Continue to use add weights and perform sets of 8-12 reps to promote muscle growth
- Introduce heavy compound lift sets
- Begin to train heavy sets with more volume

Week 9

- Continue to focus on proper form and technique in all exercises
- Increase the weight used in all exercises by 5-10% to continue getting stronger and bigger.
- Perform 3-4 sets of 3-6 reps on compound lifts with heavy weights to promote muscle growth and gain extra strength.

Week 10

- Return to higher rep work with the newly gained strength
- Add in a day specific to only working the arms to help isolate the arm muscles and give some tips and tricks.
- Emphasis on recovery after 2 weeks of heavy lifting

Week 11

- Increase the weight used in all exercises by 5-10% to continue challenging the muscles
- Perform 3-4 sets of 6-8 reps
- Increase isolation training volume
- Introducing the 6 day workout split
- Advanced drop sets
- Advanced Supersets
- Very Hard Week
- Combine elements from everything you learned for a week that will make you grow stronger Physically and mentally.

Week 12

- Rest
- This week we will talk about what you need to do to continue you to make progress going forward.
- You have graduated from the program
- If you have mad it this far you should have the principals of understanding muscle growth installed in you at a deep level.

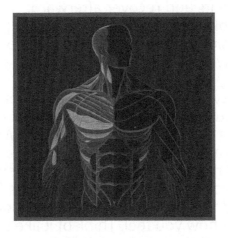

The Basics

Before diving into this 90-day workout plan, it's crucial to grasp the science behind building muscle. This book will provide you with insights, but for an in-depth understanding, consider reading my comprehensive guide, ***"The Teen's Handbook for Building Muscle and Strength."*** While we'll cover many aspects of this process throughout the plan, remember that a solid grasp of the science behind muscle building is a valuable foundation for your fitness journey.

Because you have purchased this book I would love to send you a **FREE COPY** of my book "**The Teens Handbook for Building Muscle and Strength**"

If you would like a **FREE COPY,** just email me **@raudebaughmatt@gmail.com** and let me know You bought my 90 day plan!

In your fitness journey, you can split the most crucial information into two categories: **your diet** and **your training.** These two aspects are interdependent and essential for your success in the gym. Your diet provides the fuel and nutrients your body needs to perform at its best during workouts and recover afterward.

This book will cover the training with lots of insights and progressions as we go week to week but let's talk about diet first, as we will want to make our diet as consistent as possible early on.

One key component of your diet that significantly influences muscle growth is protein. Think of **protein** as the **construction workers** for your muscles. When you engage in strength training and resistance exercises, you create tiny tears in your muscle fibers. To repair and strengthen these fibers, your body relies on the amino acids found in protein.

Try to get this protein from real food sources, what you eat will effect how you feel. Think of it like this, if you want a car to run well then put in good oil. Your body operates the same way.

Nutrition

There is a lot of bad information around muscle gain nutrition. Gaining muscle is not just work for the gym. What happens in the kitchen is equally as important. Proper nutrition is just as important as proper exercise when it comes to building muscle. In order to grow and repair muscle tissue, the body needs adequate amounts of protein, carbohydrates, and healthy fats

The Importance Of Protein

Muscle Repair
After a workout, protein helps repair the damaged muscle fibers, making them thicker and stronger than before. Every time you lift you damage your muscles and protein helps it build back slightly larger and stronger.

Protein Synthesis
Protein synthesis is the process through which your body absorbs protein to build new muscle tissue. It requires a sufficient intake of protein to be efficient.

Protein Intake
A general guideline is to aim for approximately one gram of protein per pound of body weight each day, spread evenly across four meals. This consistent protein consumption provides your body with a steady supply of amino acids necessary for muscle repair and growth.
For example a 200 lb person would want to eat 200g grams of protein a day if they are looking to gain muscle.

Protein Intake Example
- 50g from eggs and bacon in the morning
- 40g from a post workout shake
- 60g from chicken for Lunch
- 50g from fish for dinner.

This is just to give an example. I will lay out more detailed meal plans in future pages.

Protein isn't the only macronutrient; there are 2 others, Fats and carbs. Both are super important for your training and health. Meet your protein goal and to keep it simple fill the rest of your diet with healthy carbs and fats. Things like potatoes, rice, oatmeal, veggies, fruit, nut butters, olive oil, and avocados are great options.

Guidelines for Muscle Growth Nutrition

- **Consume enough protein:** Protein is essential for building and repairing muscle tissue. Aim for at least 1 gram of protein per pound of body weight per day. Good protein sources include lean meats, poultry, fish, eggs, dairy products.
- **Carbohydrates for energy and calories:** Carbohydrates are important for fueling your workouts and helping your muscles recover. Choose complex carbs like whole grains, fruits, and vegetables to provide sustained energy throughout the day.
- **Healthy fats for hormone production and calories:** Healthy fats like olive oil, avocados, nuts, and seeds help produce hormones that are necessary for muscle growth. Include a source of healthy fats with each meal.
- **Stay hydrated:** Water is crucial for transporting nutrients to your muscles, removing waste products, and regulating body temperature during exercise. Aim for at least 8 cups of water per day, and more if you're sweating heavily during your workouts.
- **Eat frequently:** Eating smaller, more frequent meals throughout the day can help regulate blood sugar levels and provide a constant source of energy for your workouts and muscle growth.
- **Timing is key:** Consuming protein and carbohydrates before and after your workouts can help maximize muscle growth and recovery. A meal or snack containing both protein and carbohydrates should be consumed within 30 minutes to 2 hours after your workout.
- **Try to eat protein 3-4 times a day to help you meet your goal:** Every time you consume protein you cause something in your body called protein synthesis to occur which is what helps your muscles grow back stronger.

Eat Enough Calories!

One of the key factors in building muscle is consuming enough calories to support growth. This means creating a caloric surplus, or consuming more calories than your body burns in a day. This surplus allows your body to use the extra energy to repair and build new muscle tissue. Let me leave this here with a quote from a famous bodybuilder and exercise scientist.

"Trying to build muscles without consuming enough calories is like trying to build a house without any bricks or wood. The protein are the builders, your workout is the blueprint and the carbs and fats are the wood and bricks, you need all 3 to cause muscle growth" - *Dr. Mike Israetel*

To gain 1 pound a week, it's important to have a caloric surplus of 500 calories a day. This means you need to consume 500 more calories than your body burns each day. This surplus can be achieved by eating more food. There are many calorie calculator tools online that can help with this.

The converse is true. If you want to **lose 1 pound per week** then you would want to **restrict 500 calories per day.** This can be made easy with cardio
200 calories from cardio + 300 from diet = a 500 deficit.
This could be necessary if you are overweight. It is possible to gain muscle and lose fat at the same time. When I started working out I lost over 75 lbs. all while gaming muscle mass at the same time. This is known as body recomposition. So If you are scrawny trying to bulk up or have a little bit of extra weight this guide will help you.

To determine the amount of calories you need for what is known as **"maintenance"** you can **multiply your body weight by 13-16.** Choose the lower end if you are not very physically active. Choose the higher end if you are extremely active. (outside or on your feet the whole day).

How physically active are you?	Body weight multiplier for maintenance level kcal
Sedative	x13
Some light activity (walk the dogs every day)	x14
Moderate activity (sports practice, outdoors for long periods)	x15
Very physically active (on your feet for 8+ hours a day)	x16

Maintenance Calories Calculator

Now that you've determined your maintenance It's important to determine whether your goal is to gain or lose weight. A key consideration in this decision is your current body composition. If you find yourself with love handles or excess stomach fat, it may be advisable to prioritize fat loss while simultaneously working on building muscle. Reducing your body fat percentage can help reveal those hard-earned muscles and create a more defined physique. On the other hand, if you already have visible abs and are relatively lean, a slow, controlled bulk might be the most suitable approach. This method can help you increase muscle mass while keeping fat gain in check, resulting in a more sculpted and muscular physique. The choice ultimately depends on your unique starting point and your specific fitness aspirations. It's crucial to tailor your approach to align with your individual goals and body composition.

Example 1.

A **200 lb. person** that is **slightly active** looking to **gain muscle** and **lose fat** at the same time would have a **maintenance calorie rate** of **200 x 14 = 2,800 Calories.** So if that same person wanted to lose **1 pound per week,** that person would need to **reduce** their caloric intake by **500 calories** a day.
 2,800 - 500 = 2,300 calories a day to lose **one pound per week** of fat while still gaining muscle.

Example 2.

Now let's look at someone that is looking to only gain weight as they are underweight and want to pack on size and bulk up.
Let's say that the person is 170 lbs. And a football player, so they are very active as they have both football practice and they are now lifting weights.
To gain 1 lb. per week. First they need to figure out their maintenance calorie rate.
170 x 16 = 2720 calories to maintain their weight.
To gain 1 lb per week they need to eat 2720 + 500 = 3220 calories EVERYDAY!

Make sense? Now it's your turn. Use the previous chart to help you find your maintenance calories per day then subtract or add 500 to gain or lose 1 pound per week.
 Please note: The weight lifting that you are going to find in this 90 day plan is factored in already to your caloric rate.

Maintenance Calories + 500 kcal. = Gain 1 lb./week

*Maintenance Calories - 500 kcal. = **Lose** 1 lb./week*

Sample Meal Plans

The following sample meal plans provided are intended as samples and can be customized to suit your individual preferences and dietary needs. Feel free to substitute foods with similar macronutrient and caloric content as desired. For instance, if you enjoy a particular meal but prefer turkey meat over chicken breast or a vegan protein alternative, that's perfectly acceptable. The key focus here is your protein intake and calorie consumption, as they are the two fundamental components to consider. Remember that food is essentially energy, and the laws of thermodynamics apply to everyone. If you consume more energy than you expend, you will gain weight, while consuming less energy than you expend will result in weight loss. Adapt these meal plans to align with your goals and preferences while keeping a close eye on your protein and calorie intake for optimal results.

Reminder, It's essential to emphasize that tailoring your protein and calorie intake to your specific body weight and your desired weight loss or gain objectives is crucial for achieving your fitness goals. The chart provided above is a valuable tool to help you determine your calorie requirements. As a general guideline, aiming for approximately 1 pound of protein per pound of body weight is a solid foundation to support your dietary needs while pursuing your goals. Remember that individual needs may vary, so feel free to adjust these values as needed to best align with your unique circumstances and objectives. By personalizing your nutrition to your body and goals, you'll be better equipped to make steady progress on your fitness journey.

Example 1. Weight Loss (2,300 Calories)

Sample Meal Plan 1

You can still gain muscle while losing weight if you are starting from a body fat percentage higher than 20% or are a beginner lifter.

Breakfast (Approx. 500 calories):
- Scrambled eggs (2 large eggs) with spinach and tomatoes (200 calories)
- Whole-grain toast (1 slice) with avocado (100 calories)
- Greek yogurt (6 oz.) with berries (100 calories)
- Black coffee or green tea (0 calories)

Mid-Morning Snack (Approx. 200 calories):
- Protein shake with whey protein (20g protein), almond milk, and a banana (200 calories)

Lunch (Approx. 600 calories):
- Grilled chicken breast (6 oz.) with quinoa (1 cup) and steamed broccoli (200 calories)
- Mixed greens salad with balsamic vinaigrette dressing (200 calories)

Afternoon Snack (Approx. 200 calories):
- Cottage cheese (1/2 cup) with pineapple chunks (100 calories)
- Almonds (1 oz.) (100 calories)

Pre-Workout Snack (Approx. 200 calories):
- Whole-grain rice cakes (2) with almond butter (2 tbsp.) (200 calories)

Dinner (Approx. 620 calories):
- Baked salmon (8 oz.) with asparagus and roasted sweet potatoes (220 calories)
- Mixed vegetable stir-fry with tofu (1 cup) (200 calories)

Evening Snack (Approx. 100 calories):
- A small serving of mixed nuts (almonds, walnuts, etc.) (100 calories)

Daily Total: Approximately 2,300 calories

Yep, you saw that right, in this hypothetical situation you could lose a pound a week and still eat 7 times a day.

Sample Weight Loss Meal Plan 2

Breakfast (Approx. 766 calories):
Breakfast (Approx. 766 calories):
- Oatmeal with sliced bananas and a drizzle of honey Peanut butter (2 tbsp) (200 calories) (500 calories)
- Scrambled eggs with egg whites (2 large eggs + half cup egg whites) (266 calories)

Lunch (Approx. 766 calories):
- Grilled chicken breast (8 oz) (180 calories)
- Steamed broccoli (1 cup) (55 calories)
- Brown rice (1 cup) (215 calories)
- Mixed greens salad with vinaigrette dressing (1 tbsp) (100 calories)
- A small piece of fruit (e.g., apple or orange) (116 calories)

Dinner (Approx. 766 calories):
- Ground beef tacos with low fat cheese (8 oz) (367 calories)
- Roasted sweet potato with a drizzle of olive oil (1 medium potato) (200 calories)
- Mixed greens salad with vinaigrette dressing (1 tbsp) (100 calories)
- Steamed mixed vegetables (e.g., carrots, green beans) (cup) (99 calories)

Snacks (Throughout the day):
- Greek yogurt (6 oz) (100 calories)
- Almonds (1 oz) (160 calories)
- Additional fruit or veggies for snacks (e.g., carrots, cucumber, or berries)

Daily Total: Approximately 2,298 calories

Sample Weight Loss Meal Plan 3

Meal 1 (Approx. 766 calories):
- Protein oats with peanut butter (1 cup of oats, 2 tbsp. peanut butter, and protein powder) (400 calories)
- Scrambled eggs with spinach (2 large eggs + spinach) (200 calories)
- A small piece of fruit (e.g., apple or banana) (166 calories)

Meal 2 (Approx. 766 calories):
- Grilled chicken breast (8 oz.) (320 calories)
- Roasted mini potatoes and mixed vegetables (1 cup) (246 calories)
- A small mixed greens salad with vinaigrette dressing (100 calories)

Meal 3 (Approx. 766 calories):
- Grilled steak (8 oz.) (450 calories)
- Brown rice (1 cup) (215 calories)
- Steamed mixed vegetables (e.g., broccoli, carrots) (1 cup) (101 calories)

Snack Before Bed (Approx. 200 calories):
- Greek yogurt (8 oz.) mixed with sugar free cheesecake mix and blueberries (200 calories)

Daily Total: Approximately 2,300 calories

Next, **we will look at people looking to bulk up and gain weight.**

Example 2. Weight Gain (3,200 Calories)

Sample Meal Plan 1

Meal 1 (Approx. 800 calories):
- Protein-packed smoothie with whey protein (1 scoop), bananas, oats, almond milk, and peanut butter (2 tbsp.) (550 calories)
- Whole-grain toast (2 slices) with additional peanut butter (2 tbsp.) (250 calories)

Meal 2 (Approx. 800 calories):
- Grilled chicken breast cooked in olive oil (8 oz.) with brown rice (1 cup) and steamed broccoli (1 cup) (600 calories)
- Mixed greens salad with olive oil (1 tbsp.) and balsamic vinegar dressing (200 calories)

Meal 3 (Approx. 800 calories):
- Fatty steak (8 oz.) with quinoa (1 cup) and sautéed mixed vegetables (1 cup) (600 calories)
- Greek yogurt (6 oz.) with honey and granola (2 tbsp.) (200 calories)

Meal 4 (Approx. 800 calories):
- Baked salmon (8 oz.) with sweet potato (1 medium) and roasted asparagus (1 cup) (600 calories)
- Mixed nuts (almonds, walnuts, etc.) (1 oz.) and a drizzle of olive oil (200 calories)

Meal 5 (Approx. 800 calories):
- Whole-grain pasta (2 cups) with lean ground turkey (8 oz.), tomato-based sauce, and olive oil (2 tbsp.) (600 calories)
- Garlic bread (2 slices) with additional olive oil (2 tbsp.) (200 calories)

Snacks (Throughout the day):
- Fresh fruit (e.g., apples, oranges, or berries)
- Greek yogurt (6 oz.)
- Cottage cheese (1/2 cup)
- Additional protein shake or bars as needed to meet daily protein goals

Daily Total: Approximately 3,220 calories

Sample Meal Plan 2

Meal 1 (Approx. 1,000 calories):
- Scrambled eggs with spinach, tomatoes, and cheese (4 large eggs) (400 calories)
- Whole-grain toast (2 slices) with butter or avocado (300 calories)
- Greek yogurt (6 oz.) with honey (2 tbsp.) (200 calories)
- Fresh fruit (e.g., a banana or an apple) (100 calories)

Meal 2 (Approx. 1,000 calories):
- Grilled chicken breast (8 oz.) with brown rice (2 cups) and mixed vegetables (1 cup) (700 calories)
- Mixed greens salad with olive oil (1 tbsp.) and balsamic vinegar dressing (200 calories)
- A serving of nuts (e.g., almonds or cashews) (100 calories)

Meal 3 (Approx. 1,000 calories):
- Baked salmon (8 oz.) with quinoa (2 cups) and roasted asparagus (1 cup) (700 calories)
- Sautéed spinach with garlic and olive oil (200 calories)
- A piece of dark chocolate for dessert (100 calories)

Snacks (Throughout the day):
- Protein shake with whey protein (1 scoop) and almond milk (1 cup) (250-300 calories)
- Greek yogurt (6 oz.) with granola (1/4 cup) (200-250 calories)
- Cheese and whole-grain crackers (e.g., cheddar and whole wheat crackers) (200-300 calories)
- Additional fresh fruit, like berries or grapes, as desired (50-100 calories each)

Daily Total: Approximately 3,000 calories

Mass Gainer Shake Recipes

Here are a few delicious shake recipes that you can incorporate into your post-workout routine to ensure you're getting the protein and calorie intake needed for muscle gain. To make these shakes, having a large blender is essential for achieving a smooth and well-mixed consistency. Investing in a quality blender, many of which are available at affordable prices on Amazon, is worth it for the convenience and versatility it offers in preparing not only shakes but also a wide variety of nutritious and satisfying meals.

I plan to make an entire cookbook, refer to my author page to get emailed about when that book is available.

Chocolate Peanut Butter Mass Gainer Shake
- 2 scoops of chocolate-flavored whey protein powder (40g protein)
- 2 tablespoons of peanut butter (200 calories)
- 1 medium banana (105 calories)
- 1 cup of whole milk (150 calories)
- 1/2 cup of rolled oats (150 calories)
- 1 tablespoon of honey (64 calories)
- Ice cubes (optional)
- Water to adjust thickness

Total Calories: Approximately 800 calories

Berry Blast Mass Gainer Shake

- 2 scoops of vanilla-flavored whey protein powder (40g protein)
- 1 cup of mixed berries (strawberries, blueberries, raspberries) (70 calories)
- 1 cup of Greek yogurt (200 calories)
- 1 cup of almond milk (30 calories)
- 1/2 cup of oats (150 calories)
- 1 tablespoon of honey (64 calories)
- Ice cubes (optional)
- Water to adjust thickness

Total Calories: Approximately 754 calories

Banana Nut Mass Gainer Shake

- 2 scoops of banana-flavored protein powder (40g protein)
- 2 medium bananas (210 calories)
- 1/4 cup of chopped walnuts (200 calories)
- 1 cup of whole milk (150 calories)
- 1/2 cup of Greek yogurt (100 calories)
- 1/2 cup of rolled oats (150 calories)
- Ice cubes (optional)
- Water to adjust thickness

Total Calories: Approximately 850 calories

The Fundamentals

In this section we will cover a few basic concepts you need to know before you start your training journey. Everything we will talk about along the way in the workout plan.

Weightlifting is a form of strength training that involves lifting weights or using resistance to challenge your muscles. This type of exercise can help you build muscle, increase your strength, and improve your athletic performance. In this section you will learn about the basics of weightlifting, including the different types of weightlifting exercises, the different muscle groups, and the importance of understanding weights and resistance levels.

If you are a healthy teen, you can expect to gain muscle and strength very fast following the steps in this book. Weightlifting is a great way for teenagers to build strength, improve athletic ability, and boost their self-esteem. Whether you are a beginner or have some experience with weightlifting, this book will provide you with the knowledge and tools you need to reach your weightlifting goals.

Muscle growth, also known as muscle hypertrophy, is the process by which muscles increase in size. It occurs as a response to increased demand placed on the muscles through resistance training exercises such as weightlifting.

When you perform resistance exercises, you put stress on your muscle fibers, causing tiny tears in the muscle tissue. In response, your body repairs the muscle tissue by adding more protein fibers, which makes the muscle larger and stronger. This process is called protein synthesis, and it's what leads to muscle growth.

Basically, your body realizes that you keep on picking up heavy things and putting them back down. As a survival mechanism your body will grow its muscles to keep up with the task to adapt you to the environment. Pretty cool right? However, it's important to note that muscle growth is a slow process and it requires consistent and progressive training. You need to gradually increase the intensity and volume of your workouts over time in order to continue challenging your muscles and stimulating growth. Additionally, adequate nutrition, rest, and recovery are also crucial components of the muscle growth process.

Muscle growth occurs as a result of the stress placed on the muscles through resistance training exercises, which stimulates the process of protein synthesis, leading to an increase in muscle size and strength.

Weight lifting + protein + healthy carbs and fats + rest and recovery = bigger muscles

Beginner Gains

WOW! Where did these muscles start to come from?! If you do everything you read in this book you will experience "beginner gains" for 1-3 years. Beginner gains means the rapid increase in muscle size and strength that individuals can experience in the first few months of starting a resistance training program. This is due to a combination of factors such as neurological adaptations, improved muscle activation, and an increase in muscle fibers.

Think of it like this. Your body is primed when you start new exercise. If you have never lifted before your body will be shocked by the stimulus of lifting. As a primal instinct, it will begin to grow to keep up with the demand placed on it from lifting. How do you make this happen? You will learn here soon.

The newness of the exercises, the use of proper form, and the body's ability to respond quickly to resistance training, all contribute to the rate of beginner gains. It is important to take advantage of these gains and build a solid foundation in the early stages of a training program, as it becomes more challenging to continue making progress as you become more advanced. Keeping track of your lifts, using proper form, and gradually increasing resistance can help ensure that you make the most of your beginner gains and continue making progress over time.

Types of Weightlifting Exercises

There are two main types of weightlifting exercises: compound exercises and isolation exercises. **Compound exercises** involve **multiple joints and muscle groups**, while isolation exercises focus on a single joint and muscle group.

Compound exercises are an efficient way to build muscle and increase strength because they challenge multiple muscle groups at once. Some **examples of compound exercises** include the **bench press, squat, overhead press, and deadlift.**

Isolation exercises, on the other hand, are used to target specific muscle groups and can help you fine-tune your muscle definition. Examples of isolation exercises include the bicep curl, tricep extension, and lateral raise. Both compound and isolation exercises can be used to build muscle in the gym.

Compound = Multiple muscles working *(Bench press uses shoulders, triceps and chest)*
Isolation = targeting one muscle *(bicep curls are only for the biceps)*

Weightlifting is a highly effective form of exercise, but it is also important to practice proper technique and safety to avoid injury and maximize the benefits of weightlifting. The importance of proper technique and safety cannot be overemphasized when it comes to weightlifting. Before starting any weightlifting program, it is crucial to learn the correct form and techniques for each exercise to avoid injury. This book will cover these topics in detail so you can create your first weight lifting plan successfully.

STOP! You can get hurt

Weightlifting and other physical exercises come with a risk of injury, and it is important to understand and accept these risks before beginning any exercise program. Before starting, please consult with a doctor or other medical professional to ensure that you are in good health and physically able to engage in weightlifting activities.

It is also important to understand and follow proper form, technique, and safety guidelines to minimize the risk of injury. Overloading your muscles, using improper form, and ignoring safety guidelines can increase the risk of injury. If you experience pain or discomfort, stop exercising and seek medical attention immediately.

The information provided in this book is intended for educational purposes only and should not be considered a substitute for professional medical advice, diagnosis, or treatment. The authors and publishers of this book are not responsible for any injuries or damages you may incur while participating in weightlifting activities.

By continuing to use this book, you acknowledge and accept the risks associated with weightlifting and physical exercise, and agree to take responsibility for your own safety and well-being.

Proper Form and Technique

Using proper form and technique is crucial when lifting weights to avoid injury and maximize the effectiveness of the exercise. For example, when performing a bicep curl, it is important to keep your elbows close to your body, move your arms in a controlled manner, and avoid swinging the weights.

To ensure that you are using proper form and technique, it is recommended that you watch videos or have a trainer or coach demonstrate the correct form for each exercise. It may also be helpful to practice with lighter weights before attempting to lift heavier weights.

Abs and Cardio

Abs and cardio are often neglected, but both are essential for overall health and fitness. Cardio helps maintain your overall health, while strong abs contribute to stability and strength throughout your body.

Abs

Here are some ab exercises for you to try as part of your routine. You have the flexibility to incorporate them into your fitness plan whenever you like, whether it's after a workout or on a separate day. Aim to do this routine **twice a week to strengthen your core and improve your abdominal muscles.** The specific exercises could include planks, crunches, leg raises, Russian twists, and bicycle crunches. You can customize the number of sets and reps based on your fitness level and goals. This does not need to be anything crazy a little bit can go a long way. Aim to keep ab workouts intense for 7-10 minuets max.

Cardio

Cardio is not required for building muscle, but I would recommend adding cardio after your workouts twice a week for general health. It can make you feel great afterward. If your goal is weight loss, however, cardio should be incorporated 2-3 times a week.

Here's an effective plan for weight loss through cardio:

Set a treadmill to 3 miles per hour at a 12-15 degree incline and walk for 20-30 minutes. Depending on your body weight, this can burn 400-500 calories in half an hour, and it only requires walking.

Warm up - Upper Body

Warming up before lifting is a critical part of any lifting routine. Warming up gradually elevates your heart rate and increases blood flow to your muscles, which helps raise your body temperature and makes your muscles more pliable. This, in turn, reduces the risk of injury by improving joint lubrication and enhancing muscle elasticity. A proper warm-up also activates the nervous system, priming it for the demands of lifting heavy weights. It mentally prepares you for the workout ahead, increasing focus and concentration.

Neglecting a warm-up can lead to strained muscles, joint injuries, and decreased performance. By taking the time to warm up properly, you not only safeguard your body but also set the stage for a more productive and effective weightlifting session.

You will do the same upper body and lower body warm ups every day. I will detail what the warm-up will be like here in-depth, and then we will include just a reminder to warm up in your actual workout plan. If you ever need a refresher on your warm-up, please return to page one to check in.

Warm-Up Routine: 5-10 minutes
Jumping Jacks
- 30-60 seconds just to get some blood pumping

Arm Swings and Circles
- Alternate between forwards and backwards arm circles, large and small.
- Swing your arms across your chest, giving yourself a hug

Bird Dog
- Begin on your hands and knees in a tabletop position.
- Simultaneously extend your right arm forward and your left leg backward. (opposite hand and foot)
- Keep your back straight and core engaged.
- Hold for 2-3 seconds, then return to the starting position.
- Repeat on the opposite side.
- Preform 10 reps each side.

Doorway Stretch (Chest Stretch)
- Stand in a doorway with your arms bent at 90-degree angles and your elbows at shoulder height.
- Place your forearms and palms against the door frame.
- Lean forward slightly to feel a stretch across your chest.
- Hold for 20-30 seconds, feeling a gentle stretch to open the chest.

Shoulder External Rotation
- Start at a cable machine with a D handle attachment at slightly above waist height.
- Hold the handle and keep your elbow and upper arm locked to your side
- Rotate the weight (2.5-5lbs) outward keeping your elbow in place rotating only from the shoulder.
- Do this for 12 reps 3 sets

Resistance Band Mobility Stretch
- Hold a resistance band at shoulder width apart.
- Bring the band over your head and behind your back feeling a stretch in the shoulders
- Return to the starting position
- Focus on keeping your arms straight and far apart to maximize the stretch.

Warm up - Lower Body

Bird Dog:
- See upper body warm up

Jumping Jacks:
- See upper body warm up
- **90/90 Hip flexor Stretch:**
- Sit on the floor with your knees bent at a 90-degree angle.
- Keep your right knee and left ankle touching the ground, while your left knee and right ankle are up.
- Lean forward slightly to feel the stretch in your hips.
- Hold for 20-30 seconds and switch to the other side.
- **Glute Bridge:**
- Lie on your back with your knees bent and feet flat on the floor, hip-width apart.
- Place your arms by your sides, palms down.
- Lift your hips off the ground by squeezing your glutes and pushing through your heels.
- Hold the bridge position for a few seconds, then lower your hips back down.
  - Repeat for 10-12 repetitions.

Leg Lifts:

- Lie on your back with your hands under your hips or by your sides.
- Lift one leg off the ground, keeping it straight.
- Lower your leg toward the floor
- This is a stretch for your hamstrings for mobility
- Perform 12-15 leg lifts, focusing on engaging your core.

Dorsi Flexion Stretch:

- Kneel on the ground with knees hip-width apart.
- Place your right foot flat on the floor in front of you.
- Position a 25 lb. weight on top of your right knee.
- Keep your heel on the ground and maintain a straight back.
- Gently lean forward toward your right foot.
- You should feel a stretch in your calf and ankle.
- Hold this position for 15-20 seconds.
- Release the stretch, remove the weight, and repeat on the other side with your left foot.

Logs and Progressing

You should log everything when you lift. For your **first few workouts** when doing a new exercise you will be doing a little **trial and error.** Here is what that could look like if your goal was to do 3 sets of 15 reps not including one warm up.

Week One Situation One

Warm up set	20 lbs. for 15 reps
Working set #1	30 lbs. for 15 reps
Working set #2	40 lbs. for 15 reps
Working set #3	50 lbs. For 15 reps

In the first scenario, you can increase the weight by 10 pounds for each set, allowing you to confidently continue adding weight next week and get in lots of stability work

Week One Situation Two

Warm up set	20 lbs. For 15 reps
Working set #1	30 lbs. for 15 reps
Working set #2	40 lbs. for 10 reps
Working set #3	30 lbs. For 15 reps

In this situation, you worked your way up to 40 pounds, and it was **too much** for you to **achieve** 15 reps. While you didn't reach the goal of 15 reps, completing 10 reps is still a commendable set for building muscle. Setting a **goal** to try the **same weight** for more reps **next week** is a good approach that indicates you're **making progress.** Following this, it's advisable to reduce the weight for the next set and perform a set within your rep goal with what you can handle. *(lighter for 15 reps on set 3)*

Overall, the **most important thing to do early on** is to **write down your workouts** and make an effort to match the sets and reps for each exercise. This way, you have a way to measure improvement and progressive overload, which involves lifting heavier weights each week. This is made possible through beginner gains, which will come quickly.

Progressive Overload

As a beginner, you'll discover that there are several methods to achieve progressive overload in your training regimen. These methods encompass **increasing the number of reps, sets, weight, and/or the intensity of your lifts.** Fortunately, starting as a beginner provides you with a prime opportunity to make rapid adaptations and efficiently incorporate these techniques into your workouts.

Going back to the week One examples I will show you a sample of what progressive overload can look like for you week to week.

Progressive Overload by Weight

Week One Situation One

Warm up set	20 lbs. for 15 reps
Working set #1	30 lbs. for 15 reps
Working set #2	40 lbs. for 15 reps
Working set #3	50 lbs. for 15 reps

Week Two Situation One

Warm up set	25 lbs. for 15 reps
Working set #1	35 lbs. for 15 reps
Working set #2	45 lbs. for 15 reps
Working set #3	55 lbs. for 15 reps

Compared to Week One, we added 5 lbs. for the same number of sets and reps in Week 2. This is an example of progressive overload.

Progressive Overload by Reps

Week One Situation Two

Warm up set	20 lbs. for 15 reps
Working set #1	30 lbs. for 15 reps
Working set #2	**40 lbs. for 10 reps**
Working set #3	30 lbs. for 15 reps

Week Two Situation Two

Warm up set	20 lbs. for 15 reps
Working set #1	30 lbs. for 15 reps
Working set #2	**40 lbs. for 13 reps**
Working set #3	30 lbs. for 15 reps

In this situation, compared to Week One, we were able to achieve more reps on the heavy set, three more reps than before. This signifies clear progress and demonstrates the concept of progressive overload. If you consistently take these small steps forward over weeks of training, they will compound into something truly impressive.

Progressive Overload by Sets

Week One Situation One

Warm up set	20 lbs. for 15 reps
Working set #1	30 lbs. for 15 reps
Working set #2	40 lbs. for 15 reps
Working set #3	50 lbs. for 15 reps

Week Two Situation One

Warm up set	20 lbs. for 15 reps
Working set #1	30 lbs. for 15 reps
Working set #2	40 lbs. for 15 reps
Working set #3	50 lbs. for 15 reps
Working set #4	50 lbs. for 15 reps

In this scenario, compared to Week One, we added an extra set in Week 2. This represents a clear progression due to more volume in your plan. These are examples of Progressive overload and you can expect to do all of these over the next 90 days. You might be surprised by how quickly your body can undergo transformations when you consistently take these small steps forward each week.

Ninety small steps forward add up to a significant leap after 3 Months.

Week One

The early weeks in this plan will focus on stability, and let me tell you, it's a game-changer for building a strong, healthy body! Stability is like the solid foundation of a skyscraper; without it, the whole thing could come crashing down. When we work on stability, we're teaching our bodies to balance and control themselves. Why is this important, you ask? Well, it's the secret to lifting heavier weights and staying safe in the gym. When you've got stability on your side, you'll find your body catching up quickly to the new heavier loads you can lift. So, remember, week one is all about building that stability – it's your ticket to becoming a gym pro!

We will introduce movements using machines in your gym this week and lots of mobility work as you will need it all for your body to be in perfect shape.

How Much To Lift?

Figuring out how much to lift as a new trainee is one of the most important steps. When determining the right weight to lift, it's important to find a balance between challenging yourself and safety. To begin, incorporating warm-up sets is crucial. Start with a lighter weight, typically around 50-60% of your intended working weight, to warm up your muscles and prepare them for the heavier load. Gradually increase the weight with each warm-up set, doing a few reps at each stage. This helps you gauge your strength and get acclimated to the movement. Once you reach a point where the weight feels moderately challenging but still manageable with proper form, you've likely found your working weight. Remember, it's a good practice to start lighter and work your way up, ensuring you avoid straining or risking injury. Over time, as you become more experienced, you can fine-tune your weight selection based on your individual goals and capabilities.

Week One Plan

- **Day One:** Upper Body
- **Day Two:** Lower Body
- **Day Three:** Rest
- **Day Four:** Upper Body
- **Day Five:** Lower Body
- **Day Six:** Rest
- **Day Seven:** Rest

Plan Logistics

Now for the logistics of this plan. To maximize your success, it's essential to review each week's workouts before heading to the gym. These workouts are intentionally designed to be progressive, introducing new concepts. Therefore, reading and studying each day's plan in advance not only ensures immediate success but also lays a strong foundation for your future fitness journey beyond this program. Be sure to write down the workouts on your phone or in a notebook advance so that you can easily access them during your training sessions. For any questions or concerns, don't hesitate to reach out to me through my author page with my email address; I'm committed to responding within 24 hours and even scheduling phone calls by appointment. Studying each workout a day in advance is crucial for understanding not just the "what" by "why" you are doing what you are doing.

You will also need to make sure you have a gym. When selecting a gym make sure you have somewhere that is easily accessible. Choose a gym that is conveniently located, whether it's near your home, workplace, or school. The easier it is to get to, the more likely you'll stick with your fitness routine.

Look for a gym that offers a variety of fitness equipment, including both free weights and machines. This diversity will allow us to create a well-rounded workout plan that caters to our stability and strength goals.

Keeping costs in check is essential. Look for options that fit your budget, whether it's a low-cost gym membership or, if you're lucky, a gym that's free for students at your school.

Check the gym's operating hours to ensure they align with your schedule. This way, you can consistently commit to your workouts without any time constraints.

REST!!

Growing muscle requires ample rest, both inside and outside the gym. Aim to rest for **at least 2 minutes between sets during your workout.** Remember, there is no rush. The more rest time you allow yourself, the better your muscles can recover and work harder. Many people don't rest long enough between sets.

Week One Day Zero

Welcome to Week One, Day zero of your transformative 90-day fitness journey! Every day along this path will come with tailored instructions for your workout. Remember, success lies in the details, so be sure to read everything carefully. Commitment and consistency are your keys to unlocking your fitness goals. Embrace the challenges, push your limits, and give it your absolute best effort. The journey may be demanding, but it's through this dedication that you'll sculpt a stronger, healthier, and more confident version of yourself. Let's embark on this adventure together and make every day count towards achieving your fitness aspirations!

Your first day in the gym may feel intimidating. Remember that nobody is judging you and most people are excited and more than happy to help. It ever hurts to just ask for help. Most people in the gym are very kind and welcoming.

Focusing on proper form over the sheer amount of weight lifted is not only for safety but also for building an effective mind-muscle connection and maximizing muscle growth. When your form is correct, you are working on the right muscle. For example if you are doing bicep curls and just swinging the weight, you are not going to grow your biceps. But if you choose something lighter and focus on the contraction you will see great results

Precise muscle activation is key for stimulating muscle growth and strength development. By prioritizing form, you ensure that the right muscles are doing the work, rather than relying on momentum or other movements.

Additionally, maintaining proper form protects against injuries, as it reduces the strain on your joints and ligaments. This allows you to train consistently and progressively over time, leading to better results in the long run. Moreover, it's easier to track your progress when your form remains consistent, making it easier to determine whether you are getting stronger or if you need to adjust your routine.

Incorporating good form into your workouts also promotes a stronger mind-muscle connection. This means you become more aware of how your muscles are working during each repetition, enhancing your ability to target and activate specific muscle groups. As a result, you'll experience more efficient muscle development and improved control over your body.

Week One, Day One - Upper Body

The first upper body workout will be all about building strength and stability in your upper body by focusing on simple pushing (think bench for push) and pulling (think row for pulling) exercises. Many of these exercises will serve as stepping stones to free weight exercises. The emphasis here is not on lifting heavy weights but on doing many repetitions to practice these movement patterns.

Remember, you should write all of this down in a notebook or on your phone after studying this workout and track everything you do.

Warmup

Please refer to the warm-up section in the book from, "Muscle Growth Basics," and complete the warm-up routine carefully before proceeding to the workout section of the book.

Workout

When you see something **written in RED** that means that it is a **new exercise.** New exercises will come with detailed instructions and tips and tricks for your workout. Whenever you **see something highlighted in red** be sure to pay extra attention to that section of the book because it will introduce new information.

- Machine Chest Press 3 sets of 12 reps
- Lat Pulldowns: 3 sets of 12 reps
- Seated Dumbbell Shoulder Press: 3 sets of 12 reps
- Dumbbell Bicep Curls: 3 sets of 12 reps
- Tricep Pushdowns: 3 sets of 12 reps

You can do MULTIPLE warm up sets. If you do 12 reps and it feels very easy again that should count as a second warmup set. (This will be true for every exercise going forward) Strive to keep 2-3 reps in reserve during your lifts. Avoid going to failure in every set, as it can hamper recovery. It might take time to grasp this sensation, but remember that strength gains can happen quickly

Machine Chest Press

The machine chest press is a stepping stone to the bench press, offering a safe and controlled environment for developing pushing strength. It adds stability with the guided motion of the machine, making it an excellent choice for beginners who need some added stability. As you become more comfortable and stronger with the machine chest press, you'll gain the confidence and muscle foundation needed to transition to free-weight exercises like the barbell and dumbbell bench press.

Execution

- Push the handles forward by extending your arms fully while exhaling. This is the concentric (positive) phase of the exercise. Visualize pushing your hands away from your chest with your chest forward and shoulders pulled back.
- Pause for a moment at the fully extended position, squeezing your chest muscles.
- Very Slowly and under control, return the handles to the starting position, inhaling as you do so. This is the eccentric (negative) phase of the exercise.
- Repeat the movement for 15 repetitions.
- You will perform 3 sets. Start with something light that you could do for a lot more than 15 reps. This is a warm up. You will follow this methods for every lift you do going forward.
- You will not count the warm up set as one of your 3 sets.
- Think about pulling your shoulders back and keeping your chest forward the whole time

Muscles Targeted   **Start**   **Finish**

Lat Pulldown

The lat pulldown primarily works the latissimus dorsi (lats) muscles, engaging them as you pull the bar down toward your upper chest, which helps in building strength and size in the back. The most important part of this exercise is engaging your back muscles and not just pulling with your arms. This takes lots of practice so do not get discouraged. You will get it

Execution

- Start by grabbing onto the lat pulldown bar while standing up.
- Place your pointer fingers on the part of the bar where the bar bends.
- Sit down with the bar in hand and fully extend your arms.
- Exhale and pull the bar to your upper chest.
- Think about leaning back slightly and pushing your chest forward.
- Pull your elbows behind your body to engage your back.
- Inhale and return to the starting position, fully extending your arms.
- Feel a stretch in your lats during this movement.
- Pro tip- think about bending the bar through your pinkies like you want to snap it on the way down

STRETCH

DRIVE ELBOWS BACK

Muscles Targeted

Start

Finish

Seated Dumbbell Shoulder Press

Seated dumbbell shoulder presses allow for a deeper range of motion compared to some other shoulder exercises. To get the most out of this exercise, start with lighter weights and gradually increase the load as you improve your form. Remember, proper form is key to prevent injury and maximize the benefits of this exercise.

Execution

- Begin by sitting on a bench with back support, holding a dumbbell in each hand at shoulder height.
- Ensure your palms are forward and in at a 45 degree angle, and your elbows are bent at a 90-degree angle.
- Exhale as you press the dumbbells upward, extending your arms overhead.
- Focus on engaging your shoulder muscles.
- Inhale and lower the dumbbells back to the starting position, maintaining control very slowly.
- Pay attention to your form and avoid arching your back.
- To optimize the exercise, think about pushing the dumbbells up as if you're trying to touch the ceiling with your palms.
- Start with lighter weights to master the movement and gradually increase the load as you become more comfortable with the exercise.

Muscles Targeted

Start

Finish

Dumbbell Bicep Curls

To work your biceps effectively, **go slow with your curls.** This keeps your biceps under tension for longer, which is crucial because biceps are small muscles. Start with lighter weights, ensure proper form, and gradually use heavier weights as you get better. This way, your biceps can keep growing.

Execution

- Start by standing with a dumbbell in each hand, arms fully extended, and palms facing forward.
- Maintain a straight posture, engaging your core for stability.
- Inhale as you curl the dumbbells toward your shoulders, keeping your upper arms stationary.
- Focus on contracting your bicep muscles as you lift the weights.
- Exhale and slowly lower the dumbbells back to the starting position, controlling the descent.
- As you reach the bottom, try to flex your triceps and think about pushing your biceps forward for an enhanced stretch.
- Avoid using momentum or swinging your body during the exercise to ensure proper form.
- To optimize this exercise, start with lighter weights, emphasizing form and control, and gradually increase the resistance as you become more comfortable.

You can substitute an EZ bar or a cable machine for dumbbells' when you see bicep curls programmed for you. It is up to personal preference and what feels the best for you. Day to day this will change so feel free to switch it up.

SQUEEZE
BICEPS
HARD

Muscles Targeted   **Start**   **Finish**

Cable Tricep Extension

Just like biceps, triceps also benefit from slow, controlled contractions and emphasizing proper form over heavy weights. Start with lighter weights, concentrate on your form, and gradually increase the resistance as you improve. This approach is effective for targeting and strengthening your triceps, which, like biceps, are smaller muscles.

Execution

- Begin by attaching a rope to a high cable pulley.
- Stand facing the machine with a firm grip on the rope, arms bent, elbows pulled into your sides, and a slight bend in your knees.
- Exhale as you extend your arms downward, focusing on contracting your tricep muscles while keeping your upper arms stationary.
- Exhale and slowly return to the starting position, controlling the upward movement.
- At the bottom of the extension, concentrate on flexing your triceps for an enhanced stretch.
- For optimal results, start with a manageable weight, prioritize feeing the contraction in your triceps at the bottom of the exercise.

YOUR ELBOWS SHOULD NEVER MOVE. Keep your elbows pulled back and stationary throughout the exercise, allowing only your forearms to perform the movement. This applies for Biceps too

| Muscles Targeted | Start | Finish |

Week One, Day Two - Lower Body

For your first lower body workout, our primary goal is to introduce you gradually to lower body exercises, emphasizing proper form and technique. The focus here is not on lifting heavy weights, but rather on familiarizing yourself with fundamental lower body movements. Again remember to log jot down how many reps you do with each weight so you can choose something more challenging for the next workout.

Warmup

Please refer to the warm-up section in the book from, "Muscle Growth Basics," and complete the warm-up routine carefully before proceeding to the workout section of the book.

Workout

- Goblet Squat: 3 sets of 12 reps
- Kettlebell Deadlift: 3 sets of 12 reps
- Walking dumbbell Lunges: 3 sets of 12 each leg
- Hamstring curls: 3 sets of 12 reps
- Dumbbell Calf Raises: 3 sets of 12 reps

You can do MULTIPLE warm up sets. If you do 12 reps and it feels very easy again that should count as a second warmup set. (This will be true for every exercise going forward)

Goblet Squat

Goblet squats are a stepping stone towards the full barbell squat. They engage the same muscle groups, with the added benefit of a lighter front load. It's a valuable exercise for building the foundation necessary to progress to more advanced squat variations.

Execution

- Hold a dumbbell with palms facing up.
- Breathe in and descend into the squat.
- Aim to have your upper leg reach parallel or deeper to the ground, as shown in the photo.
- Exhale and return to the starting position.
- Focus on opening your hips as you descend.
- Maintain even weight distribution in your feet and drive through your heels for power.

Kettlebell Deadlift

The kettlebell deadlift is a fundamental exercise for building strength in your posterior chain, including your lower back, glutes, and hamstrings. Proper technique is essential, especially for beginners. Let's break it down in a simple way:

Execution

- Stand with your feet hip-width apart, toes pointing slightly outward.
- Hinge at your hips and bend your knees to lower your body down to the kettlebell, keeping your back straight and chest up. Think about pushing your hips back on the decent.
- With a straight back and your chest up, drive through your heels to stand up.
- To lower the kettlebell back to the ground, reverse the movement by hinging at your hips, bending your knees, and maintaining a straight back.
- Lower the kettlebell back to the ground with control, making sure it lands softly to avoid any bouncing.
- Perform the desired number of repetitions, ensuring proper form and control throughout.
- The most important part is to keep your chest up and shoulders back

Muscles Targeted   Start   Finish   Start   Finish

Walking Dumbbell Lunges

Walking dumbbell lunges will help you build stability and balance in your lower body. Your warm-up set here should involve no added weight. If you have trouble maintaining you balance, consider doing a few stationary lunges while holding onto a wall for support.

Execution

- Start by standing with your feet hip-width apart.
- Take a step forward with one leg, bending both knees to create a 90-degree angle with your front thigh parallel to the ground. This will stretch your back leg's quad muscle
- Keep your back straight, engage your core, and maintain an upright chest as you step forward.
- Push through your front heel to return to a standing position, all while paying attention to the quad stretch in your back leg.
- Switch legs and repeat the lunge, walking forward with each step. This exercise helps improve leg strength and flexibility, with a focus on the quad muscles of the trailin leg.
- Focus on stretching your back quad muscle as you descend and driving your weight through your full foot i the front.
- Start light and work your way up in weight, remember to jot down all of your weights for next week.

Muscles Targeted   **Start**   **Finish**

Hamstring Curls

This compound exercise can be performed in two common variations: seated or lying down, depending on the equipment available to you. Both variations target the hamstring muscles and offer benefits for leg strength and stability.

Execution

- Lie face down or sit on a leg curl machine.
- Position your ankles under the padded lever, legs fully extended.
- Bend your knees, curl the lever toward your buttocks, and feel the hamstring contraction.
- Try not to flex your feet, as this will engage the wrong muscles, keep everything relaxed and focus on your hamstrings
- Slowly return to the starting position, fully extending your legs. Start with manageable weight, increase gradually for a safe, effective workout.

Calf Raises

The calf's are a neglected muscle by many people but are important to strengthen. Focus on slow movement and deep stretches under load with this muscle.

Execution

- Stand on a sturdy plate or two, ensuring the balls of your feet are on the plate(s).
- Hold onto dumbbells with a neutral grip, keeping your arms at your sides.
- Raise your body up onto the balls of your feet, lifting your heels as high as you can.
- Slowly lower your heels down, using the plate(s) to get a deeper calf stretch.

Muscles Targeted	Start	Finish

Week One, Day Four - Upper Body

For your second upper and lower body workouts, replicate the same exercises from day one. Review your logs from the first workouts and aim to intensify your workout as the progressive overload guidance from **page 35-38.** Add an extra set to each exercise this week, and if day one felt too simple, consider increasing the weight by 5-10 pounds in one or more sets per lift.

- **WARMUP SEE PAGE 30**
- Machine Chest Press: 4 sets of 12-15 reps
- Lat Pulldowns: 4 sets of 12-15 reps
- Seated Dumbbell Shoulder Press: 4 sets of 12-15 reps
- Dumbbell Bicep Curls: 4 sets of 12-15 reps
- Tricep Pushdowns: 4 sets of 12-15 reps

Week One, Day Five - Lower Body

- **WARMUP SEE PAGE 32**
- Goblet Squat: 4 sets of 12-15 reps
- Kettlebell Deadlift: 4 sets of 12-15 reps
- Walking dumbbell Lunges: 4 sets of 12-15 reps each leg
- Hamstring curls: 4 sets of 12-15 reps
- Dumbbell Calf Raises: 4 sets of 12-15 reps

Week One, Day Six and Seven - Rest

Rest is crucial for your progress, so don't forget to prioritize nutrition by meeting your protein goals on your rest days.

Week Two

In week two of your fitness journey, our focus will be on mastering free weight compound exercises with a strong emphasis on correct form. While it's entirely normal to be eager to lift heavy weights right from the start, it's essential to remember that proper technique is the foundation of any successful training program. So, let's leave our egos at the door and start with lighter sets. By doing so, we can effectively hone our form and get the movements right before gradually adding weight to the bar. Together, we'll embark on week two with a commitment to learning and perfecting our technique, setting the stage for safe and successful workouts in the future.

For the new exercises, follow my instructions and advice mentioned above. As for the exercises from last week, continue striving to implement overload by adding weight or increasing reps from your week one log notes.

Week Two Plan

- **Day One:** Upper Body
- **Day Two:** Lower Body
- **Day Three:** Rest
- **Day Four:** Upper Body
- **Day Five:** Lower Body
- **Day Six:** Rest
- **Day Seven:** Rest

Week Two, Day One - Upper Body

- **WARMUP SEE PAGE 30**
- Barbell bench press: 3 sets of 8 reps
- 1 arm Dumbbell row: 3 sets of 12 reps
- Lat Pulldowns: 3 sets of 12-15 reps
- Seated Dumbbell Shoulder Press: 3 sets of 12-15 reps
- Dumbbell Bicep Curls: 3 sets of 12-15 reps
- Tricep Pushdowns: 3 sets of 12-15 reps

I will provide instructions for the new exercises. For everything else, aim to **increase the weight by 5-10 pounds or do more reps than last week.** compared to last week, and keep a log of your repetitions and sets. For instance, if you managed to do 12 reps with 60 lbs during the lat pull-down exercise last week, try using 75 lbs. this time, even if you only achieve 8 reps. That's perfectly fine; just work on reaching 10 reps in your next attempt! and **LOG YOUR SETS AND REPS** so you know you are making progress.

Barbell Bench

Barbell bench press is a fundamental strength training exercise that primarily engages your upper body "pushing muscles." It involves lying on your back on a bench, lowering and lifting a barbell with weights attached to it. When you lower the barbell to your chest and then push it upward, you work your chest, shoulders, and triceps. This exercise is excellent for building upper body strength and muscle mass, making it a key component of many workout routines.

Execution

- Lie on your back on a bench with your feet flat on the floor.
- Grip the barbell with your hands slightly wider than shoulder-width apart.
- Lift the barbell off the rack and hold it over your chest with your arms fully extended.
- Lower the barbell down to your chest in a controlled manner, keeping your elbows at around a 90-degree angle.
- Push the barbell back up to the starting position, extending your arms fully.
- Repeat the movement for your desired number of reps.
- As you are new you should always have a spotter to help you if you can not complete the last rep of your set. If you workout alone just ask someone. 99/9% of people are MORE than willing to help you I promise
- It might take a few weeks to feel this in your chest and that OK.
- At all times keep your wrists straight to the arm. The common tendency is to let them bend backwards.

 When performing any pushing movement (like bench or chest press), think about starting the lift with your shoulders pulled back and your chest forward. Imagine this like you are pinching a pencil between your shoulder blades.

Muscles Targeted   **Start**   **Finish**

One Arm Row

The one-arm row is a great way to kickstart your back strength. Visualize pulling the weight by driving your elbow back and gently squeezing your shoulder blades together as you pull. This exercise not only strengthens your back but also helps improve your posture and upper body stability, making it a valuable addition to your workout routine.

Execution

- Stand with your feet shoulder-width apart, holding a dumbbell in one hand.
- Bend at your hips and knees to create a slight forward lean with your back straight.
- Keep your free hand on a bench or other support for balance.
- Slowly lift the dumbbell with the working arm, driving your elbow back and squeezing your shoulder blade.
- Lower the dumbbell in a controlled manner, allowing your arm to fully extend.
- Repeat the movement for your desired number of reps, then switch to the other arm. It's perfectly fine to take a few weeks to feel this exercise effectively targeting your back muscles. Remember to maintain proper form and gradually increase the weight as you become more comfortable with the movement.

 When performing any row exercise, the real growth comes from stretching at the bottom of the movement. Slowly lower the weight and focus on allowing the weight to pull your arm, toward the floor with each repetition.

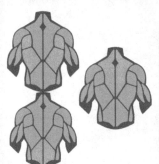

Muscles Targeted   **Start**   **Finish**

Week Two, Day Two - Lower Body

Warmup (page 30)

Remember to continue not neglecting your warm-up; this needs to be thoroughly completed before every workout to help with your mobility and injury prevention

Workout

- Barbell squat: 3 sets of 8 reps
- Romanian deadlift: 3 sets of 8 reps
- Walking dumbbell Lunges: 3 sets of 12 each leg
- Hamstring curls: 3 sets of 12 reps
- Dumbbell Calf Raises: 3 sets of 12 reps
- Leg extension: 3 sets of 12 reps

Barbell Squat

Barbell squats work all your leg muscles and are a tough exercise to get the hang of so don't get discouraged. Just stay with your training routine practice makes perfect. Squats help build leg muscles, boost testosterone (for guys), and make your lower body and core and more stable. Squats can bulk you up, so don't skip them.

Equipment Setup

Find a squat rack, and adjust the safety bars at a level where, if you go down and can't get back up, you can safely drop the weight onto the bars.

Adjust the bar so that when you extend your arms out, the bar is at around armpit height

Barbell Squat continued

Begin your workout with just the bar, and gradually increase the weight in 5-10 pound increments until performing 8 reps feels challenging. If you find that you're starting with a lighter weight and it feels very easy, you can consider adding weight in larger increments, but it's important to still focus on form. Do lots of practice sets with just the bar to ensure you understand proper form

Execution

- Approach the barbell, step under it, and place it across your upper back, resting on your trapezius muscles.
- Grasp the barbell with a firm, even grip and squeeze your shoulder blades together to create a stable platform.
- Lift the bar off the rack, take a step back, and ensure your feet are still shoulder-width apart.
- Keep your chest up, back straight, and your eyes looking forward.
- Begin the squat by opening at your hips and knees, lowering your body down as if you're sitting back into a chair.
- Go as low as your flexibility allows, ideally until your thighs are parallel to the ground or slightly below.
- Maintain a neutral spine and keep your knees in line with your toes throughout the movement.
- Push through your heels to stand back up, straightening your legs and returning to the starting position.

When performing the squat, take a video of your sets from the side to assess your form. Your hips and chest should move like an elevator and together. Do not let the hips or chest rise separately

Muscles Targeted   **Start**   **Finish**

Romanian Deadlift

Start your RDL workout with just the bar. Add more weight in 5-10 pound steps until 8 reps become challenging. If it's too easy at first, you can add more weight, but always focus on your form. Do lots of practice sets with just the bar to make sure you're doing it right. RDL is an exercise where you want to focus on **stretching your hamstrings** deep and fully at the bottom.

Execution

- Stand with feet hip-width apart, toes slightly turned outward. Hold a barbell with hands slightly wider than shoulder-width.
- Maintain a straight back throughout the movement, avoiding rounding or arching. Keep your head in a neutral position, looking forward or slightly down.
- Initiate the movement by pushing your hips back while keeping your chest up. Imagine pushing your hips toward the wall behind you. Keep a slight bend in your knees without locking them.
- As you hinge at the hips, slowly lower the barbell while keeping it close to your legs. You should feel a stretch in your hamstrings as the bar reaches below knee level.
- Reverse the movement by driving your hips forward and squeezing your glutes at the top. Maintain the straight back throughout.
- As you lower the bar, maintain control and keep it close to your body. Perform sets of 8 reps, focusing on proper technique

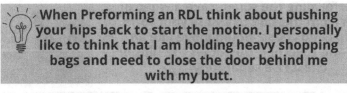 

When Preforming an RDL think about pushing your hips back to start the motion. I personally like to think that I am holding heavy shopping bags and need to close the door behind me with my butt.

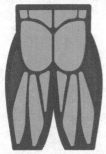  

Muscles Targeted   **Start**   **Finish**

Leg Extension

Leg extensions are an isolation exercise that targets the quadriceps in your legs. When performing leg extensions, remember to execute the movements slowly. However, you can push yourself hard in this exercise as it is one of the safest exercises but still delivers significant benefits.

Execution

- Adjust the leg extension machine to your body's size, ensuring your knees align with the machine's pivot point, and your back is comfortably supported.
- Sit on the machine with your back firmly against the backrest, and your feet hooked under the padded ankle rollers.
- Lift your legs by extending your knees until your legs are almost fully straight but not locked. Exhale during this upward movement.
- Lower your legs in a slow, controlled manner to return to the starting position, inhaling as you do so.
- Perform your desired number of reps, typically in the range of 8-12, focusing on engaging your quadriceps throughout the exercise.
- Start light and work your way up until completing 12 reps is very challenging

 Try pausing for 1-2 seconds at the top of the lift then lower the weight for 3-4 seconds. This will make using lighter weights even harder which is a good thing!

HOLD

  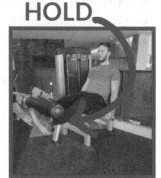

Muscles Targeted   **Start**   **Finish**

Week Two, Day Three - Rest
Week Two, Day Four - Upper Body

For your second upper and lower body workouts in week two, replicate the same exercises from day one and two of this week. Review your logs from earlier this week and aim to intensify your workout as the progressive overload guidance from **page 35-38.** Add an extra set to each exercise this week, and if day one felt too easy, consider increasing the weight by 5-10 pounds in one or more sets per lift.

- **WARMUP SEE PAGE 30**
- Barbell bench press: 4 sets of 8-10 reps
- 1 arm Dumbbell row: 4 sets of 12-15 reps
- Lat Pulldowns: 4 sets of 12-15 reps
- Seated Dumbbell Shoulder Press: 4 sets of 12-15 reps
- Dumbbell Bicep Curls: 4 sets of 12-15 reps
- Tricep Pushdowns: 4 sets of 12-15 reps

Week Two, Day Five - Lower Body

- **WARMUP SEE PAGE 32**
- Barbell squat: 4 sets of 8-12 reps
- Romanian deadlift: 4 sets of 8-12 reps
- Walking dumbbell Lunges: 4 sets of 12-15 each leg
- Hamstring curls: 4 sets of 12-15 reps
- Dumbbell Calf Raises: 4 sets of 12-15 reps
- Leg extension: 4 sets of 1215 reps

Week Two, Day Six and Seven - Rest

Rest is crucial for your progress, so don't forget to prioritize nutrition by meeting your protein goals on your rest days.

Week Three

In week three, we're all about keeping up the progress in your workouts. To do that, we're bumping up the weight by 5-10% compared to what you did last week. *For example, if you were bench pressing 95 pounds for 8 reps in week 2, this week, we're going to challenge you with a bench press at 105 pounds.* Our goal is to aim for 8 reps with this heavier weight weight. Later in the week, we'll also focus on some even heavier sets to keep you on the path to improvement.

Week Three Plan

- **Day One:** Upper Body
- **Day Two:** Lower Body
- **Day Three:** Rest
- **Day Four:** Heavy Upper Body
- **Day Five:** Heavy Lower Body
- **Day Six:** Rest
- **Day Seven:** Rest

Week Three, Day One - Upper Body

- **WARMUP SEE PAGE 30**
- Barbell bench press: 3 sets of 8 reps
- 1 arm Dumbbell row: 3 sets of 12 reps
- Lat Pulldowns: 3 sets of 12-15 reps
- Seated Dumbbell Shoulder Press: 3 sets of 12-15 reps
- Dumbbell Bicep Curls: 3 sets of 12-15 reps
- Tricep Pushdowns: 3 sets of 12-15 reps

Week Three, Day Two - Lower Body

- **WARMUP SEE PAGE 32**
- Barbell bench press: 3 sets of 8 reps
- 1 arm Dumbbell row: 3 sets of 12 reps
- Lat Pulldowns: 3 sets of 12-15 reps
- Seated Dumbbell Shoulder Press: 3 sets of 12-15 reps
- Dumbbell Bicep Curls: 3 sets of 12-15 reps
- Tricep Pushdowns: 3 sets of 12-15 reps

Attempt to increase all weights by 5-10% for **Week Three** Day One AND TWO if you miss the rep goal say *(only got 7 reps of bench press and fail on the last rep)* **that's okay** just write it down so you remember what to shoot for next week.

Week Three, Day Three - Rest

For your second upper and lower body workouts in week three, We will work up to **heavy sets of 5 reps on squat and bench!** When trying to build muscle and strength sets of 1-5 build lots of strength. This is to help you get stronger.

Take your week 2 set of 8 and add 15%. to weights For example, if you were able to bench/squat 100 lbs. for 8 last week, try doing 115 lbs. for 5 this week For just a set to test it out then drop the weight back down

For your other exercises try to increase the weight by 5-10% **OR** add in an extra set at the same weight in the 12-15 rep range. *Remember muscle growth is a result of SLOWLY lifting heavier weights over time.*

Week Three, Day Four - Upper Body

- WARMUP SEE PAGE 30
- Barbell bench press: 1 set of 5 heavier reps 2 Sets of 8
- 1 arm Dumbbell row: 3-4 sets of 12-15 reps
- Lat Pulldowns: 3-4 sets of 12-15 reps
- Seated Dumbbell Shoulder Press: 3 sets of 12-15 reps
- Dumbbell Bicep Curls: 3 sets of 12-15 reps
- Tricep Pushdowns: 4 sets of 12-15 reps

Week Two, Day Five - Lower Body

- WARMUP SEE PAGE 32
- Barbell squat: 3 sets of 5 heavy reps
- Romanian deadlift: 3-4 sets of 8-12 reps
- Walking dumbbell Lunges: 3-4 sets of 12-15 each leg
- Hamstring curls: 3-4 sets of 12-15 reps
- Dumbbell Calf Raises: 3-4 sets of 12-15 reps
- Leg extension: 3-4 sets of 12-15 reps

Week Two, Day Six and Seven - Rest

Rest is crucial for your progress, so don't forget to prioritize nutrition by meeting your protein goals on your rest days.

Week Four

In week four we are going to train hard because next week is an active recover week which means you get a rest from your weight lifting! Lets make this week count.

Try using the **same weight** you used for 5 reps on **squats and bench last week,** but this time **aim for 8 reps.** If you can't complete 8 reps in any set, reduce the weight and continue trying for 8 reps. For everything else lets increase the weight by 10-20% and drop the reps to heavier sets of 8. unless otherwise noted.

Week Four Plan

- **Day One:** Upper Body
- **Day Two:** Lower Body
- **Day Three:** Rest
- **Day Four:** Upper Body
- **Day Five:** Lower Body
- **Day Six:** Rest
- **Day Seven:** Rest

Week Four, Day One - Upper Body

- **WARMUP SEE PAGE 30**
- Barbell bench press: 3 sets of 8 reps
- 1 arm Dumbbell row: 4 sets of 8 reps
- Lat Pulldowns: 4 sets of 8 reps
- Seated Dumbbell Shoulder Press: 3 sets of 12-15 reps
- Dumbbell Lateral Raise: 3 sets of 12-15 reps
- Cable Chest Fly: 3 sets of 12-15 reps
- Dumbbell Bicep Curls: 3 sets of 12-15 reps
- Tricep Pushdowns: 3 sets of 12-15 reps

Week Four, Day Two - Lower Body

- **WARMUP SEE PAGE 32**
- Barbell squat: 3 sets of 8 reps
- Romanian deadlift: 4 sets of 8 reps
- Split Squats: 3 sets of 8 reps
- Hamstring curls: 3-4 sets of 12-15 reps
- Dumbbell Calf Raises: 3-4 sets of 12-15 reps
- Leg extension: 3-4 sets of 12-15 reps

Dumbbell Lateral Raise

Dumbbell lateral raises are an isolation exercise that targets the outside of your shoulders. This exercise helps create a broader and more three-dimensional appearance in your shoulder muscles.

Execution

- Stand with your feet shoulder-width apart, holding a dumbbell in each hand by your sides, palms facing your body.
- Maintain an upright posture with a slight bend in your elbows, and keep your back straight throughout the exercise.
- Raise both dumbbells simultaneously to the sides, keeping your arms extended but not locked, until they reach shoulder level. Your body forms a "T" shape.
- Hold the raised position briefly, focusing on the contraction of your lateral deltoid muscles.
- Lower the dumbbells slowly and with control to the start

Cable Chest Fly

The chest fly is an exercise that effectively isolates the chest. Focus on stretching at the bottom of the lift and squeezing your chest together at the top for maximum benefit.

Execution

- Stand in the middle of a cable machine with the pulleys set at chest height. Grasp a handle in each hand, one in each hand, and take a step forward with one foot to create tension in the cables.
- Maintain a slight bend in your elbows and a stable, upright posture. Keep your hands close to the center of your chest, palms facing forward, and elbows slightly bent.

- Slowly push your hands out and away from each other in a controlled, hugging motion. You should feel a stretch in your chest muscles.
- Reverse the motion and bring your hands back together in front of your chest, focusing on **squeezing** your chest muscles as you do so.

Muscles Targeted   **Start**   **Finish**

Split Squat

In this workout, split squats will replace lunges. Split squats are quite similar to lunges but involve a slightly larger range of motion, and you'll be focusing on one leg at a time. take some time to practice this with no weight for your warmup sets.

- Stand facing away from the bench, about two feet away. Hold a dumbbell in each hand, arms by your sides.
- Place your back foot, the shoelaces area, on top of the bench, while your front foot stays in front of you.
- Keep your chest up, shoulders back, and maintain a neutral spine throughout the exercise.
- Begin by bending your front knee and lowering your body down toward the ground. Keep your back knee close to the floor but do not let it touch.
- Lower your body until your front thigh is parallel to the ground or slightly below. Ensure your front knee is aligned with your ankle, not extending past it.
- Push through your front heel to return to the starting position. Focus on using the front leg to lift your body.
- Perform 8 reps for each leg in a controlled manner.

 Begin by placing the dumbbells on the ground and setting yourself up in the split squat position before descending to pick them up. Position the dumbbells near your ankle bones.

KNEE STRAIGHT DOWN

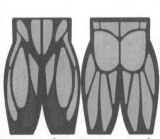

Muscles Targeted   **Start**   **Finish**

Week Four, Day Three - Rest

For the second half of week four, we are going to increase the volume (total sets). Try to maintain the weight you've been using, or if possible, increase the weight for more sets this week, as outlined below. Keep in mind that this is your last workout block before a prolonged period of rest, so make sure you give it your all. If you can increase the weight on a few lifts, that's great, but be prepared to lower the weight if your form begins to break down, especially since we are doing 5 sets for some of these exercises. Remember, prioritize form and safety over heavy weights.

Week Four, Day Four - Upper Body

- **WARMUP SEE PAGE 30**
- Barbell bench press: 5 sets of 8 reps
- 1 arm Dumbbell row: 5 sets of 8 reps
- Lat Pulldowns: 5 sets of 8 reps
- Seated Dumbbell Shoulder Press: 5 sets of 12-15 reps
- Dumbbell Lateral Raise: 5 sets of 12-15 reps
- Cable Chest Fly: 5 sets of 12-15 reps
- Dumbbell Bicep Curls: 5 sets of 12-15 reps
- Tricep Pushdowns: 5 sets of 12-15 reps

Week Four, Day Five - Lower Body

- **WARMUP SEE PAGE 32**
- Barbell squat: 5 sets of 8 reps
- Romanian deadlift: 5 sets of 8 reps
- Split Squats: 4 sets of 8 reps
- Hamstring curls: 4-5 sets of 12-15 reps
- Dumbbell Calf Raises: 4 sets of 12-15 reps
- Leg extension: 4-5 sets of 12-15 reps

Week Four, Day Six and Seven - Rest

Week Five

Good work! You've made it to week 5. This week, we will take it easy and rest as you've earned it. The goal for this week is active recovery. We will do light lifting for two days to help you practice your form. Keep these sets very light and perform them slowly. Use these light workouts to get some solid practice on your technique. Later in the week, simply focus on staying active and having some fun.

Week Five, Day One - Upper Body Recovery

- **WARMUP SEE PAGE 30**
- Barbell bench press: 5 sets of 8 reps **50% of week 4 weight**
- 1 arm Dumbbell row: 5 sets of 8 reps **50% of week 4 weight**
- Lat Pulldowns: 5 sets of 8 reps **50% of week 4 weight**

Week Five, Day Two - Lower Body Recovery

- **WARMUP SEE PAGE 32**
- Barbell squat: 5 sets of 8 reps **50% of week 4 weight**
- Romanian deadlift: 4 sets of 8 reps **50% of week 4 weight**
- Split Squats: 3 sets of 8 reps **50% of week 4 weight**

Week Five, Day's Three - Seven - Rest

During this time, your only goal is to avoid lifting any weights.
I understand it might be tempting, but the rest period is valuable for your body to adapt and relax. Throughout this period, continue to focus on stretching and improving mobility.

Additionally, aim to stay active on at least two days. Try to keep your heart rate elevated for at least 30 minutes during these days. You can achieve this by playing a sport or engaging in light cardio exercises, such as using the elliptical machine. Increased blood circulation can aid in recovery and prepare you for the upcoming weeks of your training plan.

Remember progress in the gym is 50% training and 50% what you eat. Continue to nourish your body and meet your protein goal while you are engaged in active recovery protocol.

Week Six

In week 6, we're transitioning to a 5-day workout plan, which means more exercises each day. We'll be dividing our upper body workouts into two days earlier in the week. On day one, we'll focus on pushing exercises like the bench press, where you push weights away from your body. On day two, it's all about pulling exercises, working on your back and biceps, where you pull things towards your body. Be prepared for things to intensify from here on out. Your dedication and hard work will pay off as you take on this more challenging workout routine.

Week Six Plan

- **Day One:** Push
- **Day Two:** Pull
- **Day Three:** Legs
- **Day Four:** Rest
- **Day Five:** Upper body
- **Day Six:** Lower body
- **Day Seven:** Rest

Week Six, Day One - Push

- **WARMUP SEE PAGE 30**
- Barbell Bench: 4 Sets of 8-12
- Incline Dumbbell Bench: 3 sets of 12
- Barbell Shoulder Press: 3 sets of 10-12
- Lateral Raise: 4 Sets of 8-12
- Single arm tricep extension: 3 sets of 15 each arm
- Tricep Pushdown: 3 sets of 8-12

Incline Dumbbell Bench

Incline dumbbell bench allows you to train your chest with a deeper range of motion, emphasizing your upper chest. Because you hands are separated, you can go much deeper during the exercise

Execution

- Set the bench angle for your target chest area.
- Sit with a flat back and stable feet on the bench.
- Hold dumbbells with an overhand grip, palms facing away.
- Let the dumbbells come down breaking at the elbow like a normal bench press
- Think about pushing your chest forward and keeping your shoulders back
- At the bottom try and stretch your chest deeply
- Begin with very light weights, progressively increase to a challenging set of 12 reps

SQUEEZE

Start

STRETCH

Finish

Barbell Shoulder Press

Using a barbell for the overhead press is a more compound approach, which enables you to build greater pressing strength.

Execution

- Stand with feet shoulder-width apart.
- Grip the barbell with hands slightly wider than shoulder-width, palms facing forward.
- Lift the barbell off the rack or from the floor to shoulder height.
- Press the barbell overhead in a straight line, extending your arms fully.
- Lower the barbell back to shoulder height with control.
- Maintain a stable core and upright posture throughout the exercise.
- Start with a manageable weight and progressively increase as your strength improves.

Single Arm Tricep Extension

This is an isolation exercise for the triceps, similar to the pushdown, but you perform it one arm at a time, allowing for a much deeper range of motion.

Execution

- Stand in the middle of a cable machine with the pulleys set at head height. Grasp a pully ball in one hand with no attachment.
- Keep your elbow in a fixed position and drive your elbow back the whole time
- Extend your arm fully, pushing the handle down while keeping your upper arm stationary.
- Pause briefly at the bottom of the movement.
- Extend your arm fully, pushing the handle down while keeping your upper arm stationary.
- Pause briefly at the bottom of the movement and squeeze your tricep hard.

Muscles Targeted   Start   Finish

Week Six, Day Two - Pull

- **WARMUP SEE PAGE 30**
- One Arm Row: 4 Sets of 12 reps
- Lat Pulldown: 4 Sets of 8-12 reps
- Lat Pull-in: 3 sets of 12 reps
- Bicep Curls: 9 Sets of 12 reps
  - 3 Sets of EZ bar curls reps
  - 3 sets of cable machine curls reps
  - 3 Sets of hammer Curls reps
- Face Pulls: 3 Sets of 12 reps

Hammer Curls

Keep your palms facing in like you're hitting a hammer

Lat Pull-in

The lat pull-in exercise effectively targets the latissimus dorsi muscles by stretching them at the top of the and contracting them in flexion at the bottom.

Execution

- Place the T-bar pull-down bar on a cable pulley.
- Bend your knees and extend your arms overhead with a slight elbow bend.
- Pull the bar towards your stomach, squeeze your lats.
- Slowly return to the starting position and stretch your lats as far as possible.

Face Pulls

Face pulls target the upper back and rear delts and are great for fixing rounded shoulders and posture issues

Execution

- Attach a rope handle to a high pulley on a cable machine.
- Stand facing the machine with feet shoulder-width apart.
- Grasp the handles with both hands, palms facing each other.
- Pull the rope towards your face, squeezing your shoulder blades together.
- Hold briefly at head level, feeling the contraction in your upper back.
- Slowly return to the starting position, keeping your form in check.

Week Six, Day Three - Lower Body

- **WARMUP SEE PAGE 32**
- Leg Press: 4 Sets of 12 Reps
  - *I am giving you a break from Squats this week. **Leg press** is very similar to the squat. slowly add weight on each side until 12 reps is hard Then start your 3 sets.*
- Romanian deadlift: 5 sets of 8 reps
- Split Squats: 4 sets of 8 reps
- Hamstring curls: 4-5 sets of 12-15 reps
- Dumbbell Calf Raises: 4 sets of 12-15 reps
- Leg extension: 4-5 sets of 12-15 reps

Leg Press
Drive through your heels and go slow on the way down with the weight, Avoid locking your knees

Week Six, Day Four - Rest

Week Six, Day Five - Upper Body

- **WARMUP SEE PAGE 30**
- Barbell bench press: 5 sets of 8 reps
- Seated Cable Row: 5 sets of 8 reps
- Lat Pulldowns: 5 sets of 8 reps
- Barbell Shoulder Press: 5 sets of 8 reps
- Dumbbell Lateral Raise: 5 sets of 12-15 reps
- Cable Chest Fly: 5 sets of 12-15 reps
- Dumbbell Bicep Curls: 5 sets of 12-15 reps
- Tricep Pushdowns: 5 sets of 12-15 reps

STRETCH

Week Six, Day Six - Lower Body

- **WARMUP SEE PAGE 32**
- Leg Press: 4 Sets of 12 Reps
- Romanian deadlift: 5 sets of 8 reps
- Split Squats: 4 sets of 8 reps
- Hamstring curls: 4-5 sets of 12-15 reps
- Dumbbell Calf Raises: 4 sets of 12-15 reps
- Leg extension: 4-5 sets of 12-15 reps

Squeeze

Seated Cable Row
Drive your elbows back and focus on a deep stretch at the bottom of the lift

> **Your goal for Week six, day Five and Six, is to take the last set to failure of each lift. That means that you take your last set to the point where you could not complete one more rep with good form then stop. make sure to have a spotter!**

Week Six, Day Seven - Rest

Week Seven

In week Seven, we will focus on increasing intensity if your sets. We will do this by adding in drop sets and super sets for some exercises.

Week Seven, Day One - Push

- **WARMUP SEE PAGE 30**
- Barbell Bench: 4 Sets of 8-12 reps
- Incline Dumbbell Bench: 3 sets of 12
- Barbell Shoulder Press: 3 sets of 10-12
- Front Raise: 3 Sets of 12 reps
- Lateral Raise: 4 Sets of 8-12 reps
  - Drop set your last set and go to failure.
- Single arm tricep extension: 3 sets of 15 reps each arm
  - Drop set your last set and go to failure
- Tricep Pushdown: 3 sets of 8-12 reps

Front Raise

A drop set is when you complete a set until you can no longer perform any more repetitions, and then you reduce the weight and repeat the same process. There should be NO REST in between sets.
For example, perform a 15 lb. lateral raise for 12 repetitions, then switch to 10 lb. dumbbells and continue without taking a break.

Week Seven, Day Two - Pull

- **WARMUP SEE PAGE 30**
- Seated Cable Row: 4 slightly heavier sets of 8 reps or the same weight as last week for more reps.
- Lat Pulldown: 4 Sets of 8-12 reps
  - Drop set your last set and go to failure.
- Lat Pull-in: 3 sets of 12 reps
- Bicep Curls: 9 Sets of 12 reps
  - 3 Sets of EZ bar curls
  - 3 sets of cable machine curls
  - 3 Sets of hammer Curls
  - Choose 2 sets of biceps to preform a drop set on.
- Face Pulls: 3 Sets of 12 reps
- Dumbbell Shrugs: 3 Sets of 12 reps

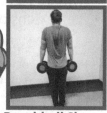

Dumbbell Shrugs
Keep your shoulders pulled back and go slowly

Day Three and Five will introduce pause reps. Pause reps mean you hold at the bottom for 2 seconds before finishing the rep. Be sure to come to a complete stop before counting to 2.

Week Seven, Day Three - Lower Body

- **WARMUP SEE PAGE 32**
- Barbell Squat Pause Reps: 4 sets of 8 reps
- Romanian deadlift: 5 sets of 8 reps
- Split Squats: 4 sets of 8 reps
- Hamstring curls: 4-5 sets of 12-15 reps
- Dumbbell Calf Raises: 4 sets of 12-15 reps
- Leg extension: 4-5 sets of 12-15 reps

Pause Rep

Week Seven, Day Four - Rest

Week Seven, Day Five - Upper Body

- **WARMUP SEE PAGE 30**
- Barbell bench press Pause Reps: 5 sets of 8 reps
- 1 arm Dumbbell row: 5 sets of 8 reps
- Lat Pulldowns: 5 sets of 8 reps
- Barbell Shoulder Press: 5 sets of 8 reps
- Dumbbell Lateral Raise: 5 sets of 12-15 reps
- Cable Chest Fly: 5 sets of 12-15 reps
- Dumbbell Bicep Curls: 5 sets of 12-15 reps
- Tricep Pushdowns: 5 sets of 12-15 reps

Week Seven, Day Six - Lower Body

- **WARMUP SEE PAGE 32**
- Leg Press: 4 Sets of 12 reps
- Romanian deadlift: 5 sets of 8 reps
- Split Squats: 4 sets of 8 reps
- Hamstring curls: 4-5 sets of 12-15 reps
- Dumbbell Calf Raises: 4 sets of 12-15 reps
- Leg extension: 4-5 sets of 12-15 reps

Your goal for Week Seven, day Five and Six, is to increase the weight you are using, sets preformed, or do more reps from what you have loggeed from day 1-3 refer to page 36 if you need help

Week Seven, Day Seven - Rest

Week Eight

In week 8, we will attempt heavy sets of squats and bench presses (3-4 reps), really pushing ourselves. For everything else, we will continue to train with intensity and perform lots of sets. The emphasis for this week and the next will be on building strength.

Week Eight, Day One - Push

- **WARMUP SEE PAGE 30**
- Barbell Bench: 3 HEAVY sets of 3-4 reps
- Incline Dumbbell Bench: 3 sets of 12 reps
- Barbell Shoulder Press: 3 sets of 10-12 reps
- Front Raise: 3 Sets of 12 reps
- Lateral Raise: 4 Sets of 8-12 reps
  - Drop set your last set and go to failure.
- Single arm tricep extension: 3 sets of 15 reps each arm
  - Drop set your last set and go to failure
- Tricep Pushdown: 3 sets of 8-12 reps
- Machine Chest Press Burnout: **only do one set but drop set 2 times to failure**

If you do your first "Heavy" set of 3-4 and think that you have more to give, log your set and try increasing the weight. The goal here is to do 3 challenging sets of 3-4 reps. As always, log your weight, sets, and reps for next time, as we will be attempting to do the same weight for more reps.

Week Eight, Day Two - Pull

- **WARMUP SEE PAGE 30**
- Seated Cable Row: 5 sets of 8 reps
- Single Arm Pulldown: 4 Sets of 12 reps
- Lat Pull-in: 3 sets of 12 reps
- Bicep Curls: 9 Sets of 12 reps
  - 3 Sets of EZ bar curls
  - 3 sets of cable machine curls
  - 3 Sets of hammer Curls
  - Choose 2 sets of biceps to preform a drop set on.
- Face Pulls: 4 Sets of 12-15 reps
- Dumbbell Shrugs: 4 Sets of 12-15 reps

Single Arm Pulldown
This should be similar to a conventional lat-pulldown but gives you the chance to work one side at time to help counter and imbalances Focus on driving your elbow behind you and squeezing your back.

Week Eight, Day Three - Lower Body

- **WARMUP SEE PAGE 32**
- Barbell Squat: 3 HEAVY sets of 3-4 reps
- Romanian deadlift: 5 sets of 8-12 reps
- Split Squats: 4 sets of 8-12 reps
- Hamstring curls: 4-5 sets of 12-15 reps
  - Drop Set on your last set and go to failure
- Dumbbell Calf Raises: 4 sets of 12-15 reps
- Leg extension: 4-5 sets of 12-15 reps
  - Drop Set on your last set and go to failure

Week Eight, Day Four - Rest
Week Eight, Day Five - Upper Body

- **WARMUP SEE PAGE 30**
- Barbell bench press: 3 Sets of 5 reps *(same weight for more reps than day one)*
- Single Arm Pulldown: 5 sets of 8 reps
- Lat Pull in: 5 sets of 8 reps reps
- Barbell Shoulder Press: 5 sets of 8 reps
- Dumbbell Lateral Raise: 5 sets of 12-15 reps
- Cable Chest Fly: 5 sets of 12-15 reps
- Dumbbell Bicep Curls: 5 sets of 12-15 reps
- Tricep Pushdowns: 5 sets of 12-15 reps

Week Eight, Day Six - Lower Body

- **WARMUP SEE PAGE 32**
- Barbell squat: 3 Sets of 5 *(same weight for more reps than day one)*
- Romanian deadlift: 5 sets of 8 reps
- Split Squats: 4 sets of 8 reps
- Hamstring curls: 4-5 sets of 12-15 reps
- Dumbbell Calf Raises: 4 sets of 12-15 reps
- Leg extension: 4-5 sets of 12-15 reps

Your goal for Week Eight, day Five and Six, is to increase the weight you did on your heavy bench and heavy squat earlier in the week. For example if you were able to bench 135 lbs. for 3 sets of 4 try it for 3 sets of 5. (adding reps)

Week Eight, Day Seven - Rest

Week Nine

In Week 9, we'll stick to the same workout plan as Week 8. On your first day for bench and squat, go for a heavy set. (heavier than last week) On the second day, try the same weight and aim for more reps. Doing the same exercises week to week is on purpose and it helps your muscles grow. Keep adding weight and doing more reps when you can. Getting really good at a few lifts is 100x better than trying to have too much variety. Keep pushing!

Week Nine, Day One - Push

- **WARMUP SEE PAGE 30**
- Barbell Bench: 3 HEAVY sets of 3-4 reps
- Incline Dumbbell Bench: 3 sets of 12 reps
- Barbell Shoulder Press: 3 sets of 10-12 reps
- Front Raise: 3 Sets of 12 reps
- Lateral Raise: 4 Sets of 8-12 reps
  - Drop set your last set and go to failure.
- Single arm tricep extension: 3 sets of 15 each arm reps
  - Drop set your last set and go to failure
- Tricep Pushdown: 3 sets of 8-12 reps
- Machine Chest Press Burnout: **only do one set but drop set 2 times to failure**

Week Nine, Day Two - Pull

- **WARMUP SEE PAGE 30**
- Seated Cable Row: 5 sets of 8 reps
- Single Arm Pulldown: 4 Sets of 12 reps
- Lat Pull-in: 3 sets of 12 reps
- Bicep Curls: 9 Sets of 12 reps
  - 3 Sets of EZ bar curls
  - 3 sets of cable machine curls
  - 3 Sets of hammer Curls
  - Choose 2 sets of biceps to preform a drop set on.
- Face Pulls: 4 Sets of 12-15 reps
- Dumbbell Shrugs: 4 Sets of 12-15 reps

Week Nine, Day Three - Lower Body

- **WARMUP SEE PAGE 32**
- Barbell Squat: 3 HEAVY sets of 3-4 reps
- Romanian deadlift: 5 sets of 8-12 reps
- Split Squats: 4 sets of 8-12 reps
- Hamstring curls: 4-5 sets of 12-15 reps
  - Drop Set on your last set and go to failure
- Dumbbell Calf Raises: 4 sets of 12-15 reps
- Leg extension: 4-5 sets of 12-15 reps
  - Drop Set on your last set and go to failure

Week Nine, Day Four - Rest
Week Nine, Day Five - Upper Body

- **WARMUP SEE PAGE 30**
- Barbell bench press: 3 Sets of 5 *(same weight for more reps than day one)*
- Single Arm Pulldown: 5 sets of 8
- Lat Pull in: 5 sets of 8 reps
- Barbell Shoulder Press: 5 sets of 8 reps
- Dumbbell Lateral Raise: 5 sets of 12-15 reps
- Cable Chest Fly: 5 sets of 12-15 reps
- Dumbbell Bicep Curls: 5 sets of 12-15 reps
- Tricep Pushdowns: 5 sets of 12-15 reps

Week Nine, Day Six - Lower Body

- **WARMUP SEE PAGE 32**
- Barbell squat: 3 Sets of 5 *(same weight for more reps than day one)*
- Romanian deadlift: 5 sets of 8 reps
- Split Squats: 3 sets of 8 reps
- Lunges: 2 sets of 20 reps each leg
- Hamstring curls: 4-5 sets of 12-15 reps
- Dumbbell Calf Raises: 4 sets of 12-15 reps
- Leg extension: 4-5 sets of 12-15 reps

You are in the thick of your training. You have learned the form, you have been making progress; this is where you have to put your head down and try to get a little better each week. Practice with intention and make every rep of every set count.

Week Nine, Day Seven - Rest

Week Ten

In Week 10, we will take a break from the heavy sets. Those sets of 4 reps will take a toll on you. After you graduate from this plan and use these systems to make progress, you need to know when to let your body recover. This week, we will be adding an arm day as well, which is always a fun workout when you're trying to recover from some heavy sets as arms do not require any crazy heavy loads. Get ready for the craziest pump of your life with arm day!

Week Ten Plan

- **Day One:** Chest and Back
- **Day Two:** Arms and Shoulders
- **Day Three:** Lower Body
- **Day Four:** Rest
- **Day Five:** Upper Body
- **Day Six:** Lower Body
- **Day Seven:** Rest

Week Ten, Day One - Chest and Back

Today we will introduce a super set. a superset is preforming an exercise and preforming a different exercise right after it and alternating back and forth. For example in day one here you will do Dumbbell bench then dumbbell row, dumbbell bench then dumbbell row etc. **Alternating back and forth**

- **WARMUP SEE PAGE 30**
- Dumbbell Bench: 3 sets of 8 reps
    - **Super set with -** Dumbbell Row: 3 Sets of 12 reps
- Cable Chest Flys: 4 sets of 12 reps
    - **Super set with -** Lat Pull in 4 sets of 12 reps
- Machine Chest Press: 3 sets of 8-15 reps. (push really hard)
    - **Super Set with -** Dumbbell Reverse Fly: 3 sets of 12 reps
- Wide Pushup: 3 Sets of 8-15 (*your performance here will vary if a pushup is too hard drop to your knees*)
    - **Super set with -** Smith Machine Row: 3 sets of 12 reps

This split is known as an 'Arnold split,' where you train chest and back on the same day, then focus on arms on a separate day. Training like this for a few weeks is a great way to prioritize increasing the size of your arms. Training arms when they are fatigued, such as after heavy benching, can lead to fewer gains in the arms.

Dumbbell Reverse Fly

This isolation exercise primarily targets the rear deltoids, helping to strengthen and define the upper back and shoulder muscles.

- Sit forward on a bench, in This instance we will be super setting so you can do these right off of the Chest Press Machine
- With palms facing inward, slowly lift the dumbbells out to the sides, away from your body. Focus on using your shoulder blades to perform the movement and maintain a slight bend in your elbows.
- At the top of the movement, pause briefly and squeeze your shoulder blades together to maximize the contraction in your rear deltoids.
- Lower the dumbbells back down to the starting position in a controlled manner, avoiding any swinging or jerking motions.
- Aim for a moderate number of repetitions, ensuring proper form throughout. Increase weight gradually as your strength and comfort with the exercise improve.
- Maintain a slight bend in your elbows throughout the movement to reduce stress on the joints.

Smith Machine Row

This compound exercise primarily targets the muscles of the upper back, including the latissimus dorsi, rhomboids, and traps, while also engaging the bicep

- Stand facing the Smith machine with your feet shoulder-width apart. Position the around knee level, and load it with the desired weight plates.
- Grasp the bar with an overhand grip (palms facing down), slightly wider than shoulder-width apart. Hinge forward and maintain a straight back and a slight bend in your knees.

- Initiate the movement by retracting your shoulder blades and pulling the bar towards your lower chest.
- At the top of the movement, squeeze your shoulder blades together

| Muscles Targeted | Start | Finish |

Week Ten, Day Two - Arms

- **WARMUP SEE PAGE 30**
- Dumbbell Bicep Curls: 4 sets of 12 reps
- Tricep Extensions: 4 sets of 12 reps
- Dumbbell Shoulder Press: 4 sets of 10 reps
- Hammer Curls: 3 sets of 12 reps
- Skull Crushers: 3 sets of 10 reps
- Lateral Raises: 4 sets of 15 reps
- Single arm cable curls: 3 sets of 15 reps per arm

Skull Crushers

Elbow stays in place

Muscles Targeted | Start | Finish

Very slow stretch on the way down

Single Arm Cable Curls

Muscles Targeted | Start | Finish

Week Ten, Day Three - Legs

- **WARMUP SEE PAGE 32**
- Leg Press: 4 Sets of 12 reps
- Romanian deadlift: 5 sets of 8 reps
- Split Squats: 4 sets of 8 reps
- Hamstring curls: 4-5 sets of 12-15 reps
- Dumbbell Calf Raises: 4 sets of 12-15 reps
- Leg extension: 4-5 sets of 12-15 reps

Week Ten, Day Four - Rest
Week Ten, Five - Upper Body

- Dumbbell Bench: 3 sets of 8 reps
  - **Super set with -** Dumbbell Row: 3 Sets of 12 reps
- Hammer Curls: 3 sets of 12 reps
  - **Super set with -** Skull Crushers: 3 sets of 10 reps
- Barbell Overhead Press: 4 Sets of 12
- Dumbbell Incline Bench: 3 sets of 8 reps
- Lat Pull-in: 4 sets of 12 reps
  - **Super set with-** Cable Fly: 4 Sets of 12 reps
- Lat Pulldown: 4 Sets of 8 reps

Week Ten, Day Six - Lower Body

- **WARMUP SEE PAGE 32**
- Leg Press: 4 Sets of 12 reps
- Romanian deadlift: 5 sets of 8 reps
- Split Squats: 4 sets of 8 reps
- Hamstring curls: 4-5 sets of 12-15 reps
- Dumbbell Calf Raises: 4 sets of 12-15 reps
- Leg extension: 4-5 sets of 12-15 reps

Week Ten, Day Seven - Rest

This week, I hope you enjoyed a break from barbell bench and barbell squat. You can still have a great workout without them. It's important to take breaks from heavy lifting with barbells from time to time, especially after a few weeks of intense benching and squatting. Next week, we'll return to barbell bench and squat, but we'll aim for higher reps. Now that you're stronger, the weight you'll use will be higher than before.

Week Eleven

In Week Eleven, we'll keep increasing reps. Review what you did for bench and squat on Week 9's last heavy day. **Aim to add 2-3 reps** to that total. You heard me right. You might surprise yourself with your increasing strength.

For example if you managed to do 135 for sets of 5 reps in **week 9** aim to do **135 for sets of 6- 8 this week.**

Later in the week, we'll revisit Days one through three. Aim for the same sets and reps, but concentrate on enhancing your form for each lift. This might involve slowing down during the negative phase of your lifts or emphasizing the mind-muscle connection. It's your first time trying a 6-day split, which happens to be one of the most common workout plans for six days.

Week Eleven Plan

- **Day One:** Push
- **Day Two:** Pull
- **Day Three:** Legs
- **Day Four:** Push
- **Day Five:** Pull
- **Day Six:** Legs
- **Day Seven:** Rest

Week Eleven, Day One - Push

- **WARMUP SEE PAGE 30**
- Barbell Bench: 4 Sets of 6-8 reps *(Look at week 9 weight and add reps)*
- Barbell Overhead Press: 4 Sets of 6-8 reps *(Look at week 9 weight and add reps)*
- Skull Crushers: 4 Sets of 8-12 reps
  - **SUPERSET WITH** Front Raise: 4 Sets of 15 reps
- Dumbbell Incline Bench: 3 Sets of 8 reps
- Tricep Pushdowns: 4 Sets of 12-15 reps
  - Lateral Raises: 4 Sets of 12-15 reps

When training, prioritize progressive overload on compound exercises like bench, squat, and RDL, by writing down your sets and reps. For isolation exercises like bicep curls, sometimes you can achieve overload by training to failure across multiple sets. Keep a focus on enhancing your mind-muscle connection during these exercises.

Week Eleven, Day Two - Pull

- Smith Machine Row: 4 Sets of 10-12 reps
- Single Arm Pulldown: 4 Set of 10-12 res
- Bicep Hammer curls: 3 Sets of 8 reps
  - Superset with Dumbbell Reverse Fly: 4 sets of 15 reps
- Single Arm Dumbbell Rows: 4 Sets of 8 reps
- Single Arm Bicep Curls: 4 Sets of 12 reps
- Seated Cable Row: 3 Sets of 10-12 reps
  - **Drop Set Last Set**
- Lat Pull-in: 3 Sets of 8 reps
  - **SUPERSET WITH** Dumbbell Twist curls (At the top twist the dumbbells to activate the biceps extra **USE A VERY LIGHT WEIGHT**)

Week Eleven, Day Three - Lower Body

- **WARMUP SEE PAGE 32**
- Squats: 4 Sets of 6-8 reps *(Look at week 9 weight and add reps)*
- Romanian deadlift: 4 sets of 6-8 reps *(Go heavy here but keep proper form with your back straight)*
- Split Squats: 4 sets of 8-10 reps
- Hamstring curls: 4-5 sets of 12-15 reps
- Dumbbell Calf Raises: 4 sets of 12-15 reps
- Leg extension: 4-5 sets of 12-15 reps
  - **SUPERSET WITH:** Sissy Squats ONLY ON LAST SET 12 reps

Sissy Squats

- Stand upright, feet hip-width apart.
- Lean backward, and go up on your toes
- Bend knees, lowering body as far as comfortable.
- Engage quads, extend knees to return to start.
- Focus on controlled movements for quads.

Week Eleven, Day Four-Seven - See Below

For days 4, 5, and 6, repeat the workouts from days 1, 2, and 3, then rest on day 7. Aim to lift the same weight or even more than earlier in the week. Concentrate on improving form, executing slower reps, and enhancing the mind-muscle connection. This should be a week of very hard workouts. Push yourself as hard as possible

Week Twelve

Congratulations on completing each week of workouts! Throughout this journey, you've delved into understanding how your body moves and the intricacies of the muscle growth process. While 90 days won't turn you into a Mr. Olympia contender, it lays the foundation for a lifelong system enabling continuous muscle growth. Consistency is key— showing up at the gym month after month, year after year, is the true essence in the grand scheme. This isn't the end; it's a stepping stone, and I hope you've already witnessed some incredible results. Don't relent now—keep pushing forward and never give up!

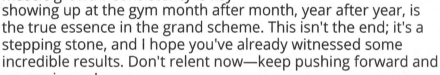

At the end of your first 90 days of lifting, your key takeaways should highlight the equivalence of diet and training, particularly the significance of protein intake. Prioritize form and the mind-muscle connection during lifts, gradually increasing weights as your body adapts for progressive overload and muscle gain. You can achieve this by adding sets and reps or by training harder with improved form week by week. *Please consider leaving a review on amazon to help other customers who are interested in this book and help me to continue to produce content if you are so willing!*

With consistent training, anyone can aim to bench press 225, squat 315, and deadlift 405 after approximately two years of dedicated effort and I would love to help you with this goal.

If this book has been helpful and you'd like to continue our training journey together, I'd love to assist you further. I'll have intermediate and advanced courses available, as well as options for affordable one-on-one training with me which includes customized workout plans for your needs. Please feel free to reach out via email. Without further closure, I wish you the best of luck in your training journey and hope to meet with you soon!

✉ RaudebaughMatt@gmail.com

I Need Your Help

Point your phone above and scan the QR code. It will take you to my amazon review page.

I would love your honest feedback so I can continue to make better books. As an independent publisher your feedback helps me so much. Thank you!

Made in the USA
Monee, IL
30 November 2024

71623188R10049